Have you ever played a "lucky" hunch? Ever had a dream come true? Received a call or letter from someone you "just happened" to think of? Felt that "I've been here before" sensation known as *Deja vu*? Sensed what was "about to happen" even an instant before it occurred? Known what someone was about to say—or perhaps even spoken the exact words along with him?

THEN YOU MAY BE USING YOUR SIXTH SENSE —YOUR ESP—WITHOUT EVEN REALIZING IT!

Recent research indicates that almost everyone possesses latent ESP powers. Moreover, those powers within you can be developed and improved. Telepathy, for example, is a talent nearly everyone has to a certain degree. And telepathic ability can be improved with training and practice! New frontiers are being opened in the understanding of ESP as man continues to explore the vast universe of the mind. Here is a challenging new look at the phenomenal field of parapsychology that not only gives you a better understanding of this mysterious and wonderful power of mind over time and matter, but also shows you how to test your own ESP ability.

ESP
YOUR SIXTH SENSE

Brad Steiger

AWARD BOOKS   •   NEW YORK

AWARD BOOKS

First printing, 1966

AWARD BOOKS are published by
Universal Publishing and Distributing Corporation
800 Second Avenue, New York, New York 10017

Manufactured in the United States of America

CONTENTS

1.

EXPLORING INNER SPACE

There are among us those who do not believe that the Age of Adventure has passed simply because all of the continents have been charted, Mt. Everest has been scaled, and the planet Earth has been orbited by manned space flight.

These new adventurers believe that an examination of the other side of man is more important than a photograph of the other side of the moon and that it is more vital to explore the "inner space" within each of us than to expend our energies and finances charting an outer space which will belong to a select few.

These scientific heretics contend that man and mind are something other than physical things. They explore matters that often contradict known physical laws, examine phenomena which do not fit into recognized bodies of knowledge, and stoutly insist that these now unexplainable events will someday be found to fit into the total scheme of nature.

These men and women devote their lives and energies to the "orphan science" called parapsychology.

The parapsychologist deals with a world that lies beyond the five senses and the reach of the physical sciences. It is a strange world where effect often precedes cause, where mind often influences matter, where individuals communicate over great distances without physical aids.

The parapsychologist makes a contribution to man's unquenchable need to know himself and the true nature of the life and the universe of which he is a part. If such parascientific phenomena as the projection of the astral self, the ability to glimpse the future, the talent to restore the past, or the facility to convey telepathic impressions are established, the boundaries of Man's universe become limitless. It will be seen—as the mystic has forever maintained—that imprisoned within each of us is all that is necessary to unlock all of life's mysteries.

Unfortunately, or perhaps fortunately, the conscious minds of the great majority of men seem unable to draw upon such knowledge even though it may be implanted within them. That for many individuals the ability to utilize this deeper knowledge can become more than a latent power has been proven through exhaustive laboratory experiments, which have amassed enough statistics to allow extrasensory perception (ESP) to become the phenomena of parapsychology which come the nearest to being accepted by the more conventional scientist.

ESP is defined by parapsychologists as the acquisition by a human or animal mind of information which it could not have received by normal, sensory means. There are some researchers, however, who take issue with the term "extrasensory perception." They protest that the phenomena may not be "perception" at all, as the receiver of this information does not know if the knowledge is right or wrong when he first perceives it. It takes a corroborating incident to convince anyone that he has perceived anything via extrasensory means.

Some parapsychologists prefer to say "paranormal cognition," but this term is subject to the same sort of criticism if the receiver is not instantly certain of the validity of the information. Besides, the researchers insist that the material in their field will eventually merge with present day physics, so the very adjective "paranormal" may be considered a misnomer.

To avoid such criticism, the current trend in parascientific research seems to be to include all of the individual classifications (i.e. precognition, poltergeists, clairvoyance, telepathy) and all related phenomena under the non-committal term "psi." Because of the wide usage of the term ESP, however, and as long as we do not make any philosophical commitment to any theory of its nature, we shall use both terms interchangeably in this book.

According to current laboratory work with such phenomena, nearly everyone has ESP. Perhaps, as children, many of us utilize extrasensory perception to a considerable degree, but, as we mature, we tend to inhibit these subconscious faculties or allow them to atrophy.

Eric J. Dingwall and John Landon-Davies, in their book, *The Unknown—Is It Nearer?*, write that their accumulated evidence indicates "everybody has ESP, but in most people it has been completely repressed in favor of normal means of perception."

Many parapsychologists, psychologists, and anthropologists, including Sigmund Freud, have theorized that telepathy may have been "the original archaic method by which individuals understood one another." As a better means of communication, which could be readily intelligible to the sensory organs, evolved, Freud conjectured, the original archaic methods were pushed into the background of man's subconscious where they may still persist, waiting to manifest themselves under certain conditions. It is obvious to all "psi" researchers that some individuals, functioning largely according to their moods and psychic needs, are able to draw upon their latent ESP abilities. Some gifted individuals are even able to make regular and practical use of the seemingly rare powers of "psi."

On June 30, 1958, Mr. Gerard Croiset, the clairvoyant whose fame has spread far beyond the borders of his native Holland, received a long-distance telephone call from a Mr. Jansen, skipper of the *Maria Judith*.

Skipper Jansen complained to Croiset that he had lost patience with a team of specialists who had been trying for weeks to pin-point the trouble spot in his diesel engine.

"I'm in the harbor here at Awijndrecht," Jansen told Croiset. "I have to sail to earn my living. I have just bought this new engine, but it does not function effectively, and the engineers can't find the trouble. What I want to know is this: must I buy a new engine? I can't sit here any longer."

Across long-distance wire and speaking to a man he had never met, Croiset was able to describe to the seaman exactly where the trouble lay. Because Croiset has very little knowledge of things mechanical, he was forced to use figurative language and comparisons in his diagnosis of the engine's trouble spot. As if he were actually on board the *Maria Judith,* Croiset told Jansen: "I go to the engine room downstairs. There I see the engine. At the back there is a small fitted pipe which makes me think of the siphon of a water-closet. That pipe has a hole in it. The reason why the engineers have not been able to find it is that you can only find this hole when the engine is hot."

Two days later, after Jansen and the engineers had completed their inspection, the skipper called Croiset and told him that his long-distance diagnosis had been correct. It had been the siphon that leaked. There had been a crack in the cylinder head. The engineers had not found the crack before, because, as Croiset had said, the engine had needed to be heated to working temperature.

The practical Dutch have long made regular use of their sensitives in much the same manner as the technically minded American would not hesitate to call in a specialist with a more conventional talent.

On April 26, 1956, Mr. P. van Delzen, a sensitive who resides in Amsterdam, was handed a photograph by a distressed resident of the city.

"It is my brother-in-law," the man told him. "He has been missing since the morning of April 23rd. In his car he left a note saying that he was planning to drown himself. Where . . . where may we find his body?"

The sensitive ran his hands lightly over the photograph of the missing man. "He is not dead," van Delzen said. "Your brother-in-law is incapable of committing suicide. He did not go into the water. He went north."

The next day, van Delzen received another call from the man. The brother-in-law had not yet been located. The family was more certain than before that the man had committed suicide.

The sensitive persisted: "Do not be alarmed. He will soon return. He is not dead."

On April 28th, the missing man called home and shame-facedly asked if the family would forgive his indiscretion. He had been depressed, had decided to run away from home, and had been working for a farmer in a village north of Amsterdam since his disappearance six days before.

While our own "psi" experiences may not be so dramatic as these, nearly all of us have had glimpses into the world of ESP. Feeling that we have been present at some previous time in a room we know we have never before entered . . . Dreaming of a friend from whom we have not heard in months, then receiving a letter from that person in the next morning's mail . . . Hearing a telephone ring and being so certain of the identity of the caller that we call him by name the instant we lift up the receiver . . .

These incidents are so common that they receive little more than half-joking comment. It is only when a paranormal event of shocking or dramatic impact startles our emotions that we relate it to others and, perhaps, even record it.

"Psi" activity is sub-divided into many types, each with a name of its own.

Precognition is that strange function of mind whereby the percipient seems to receive a glimpse of the future and gains knowledge of events yet to take place.

Telepathy is the transference of thought from one mind to another. Distance and time seem unable to affect this "psi" phenomenon. Laboratory tests have been conducted with the subject at distances of over 500 miles from the experimenter with no drop in the subject's scoring rate. An extremely impressive series of tests was carried out with the agent in the United States and the percipient in Yugoslavia.

Clairvoyance is the awareness, without physical aids or normal sensory means, of what is going on elsewhere. We have already seen how effectively Croiset "found" the leak in the cylinder head when he was over one hundred miles from a troublesome engine he had never seen.

Telekinesis is the movement of objects, seemingly caused by some force unknown to physical science.

Psychokinesis, the direct action of mind on matter, is the parapsychologists' current nominee as the culprit involved in poltergeist cases—those bizarre occurrences when bottles and crockery float through the air, fires break out on living room tables, gasoline pours out of walls, or disembodied voices cackle threats and obscenities.

Astral Projection, or out-of-the-body experience, is the apparent projection of the mind from its fleshly domicile. Such experiences may be accomplished within a small range, such as the woman in London who arose to shut off the light in the hall and was shocked to discover, as she returned to bed, that her body had never left the comfort of the bedclothes; or quite limitless, such as the monk who was seen by witnesses both in his cell in the monastery and at the bedside of the dying Pope at precisely the same moment.

Psychometry is the determining of facts about an object's owner simply from contact with the object.

Even from these brief definitions, it becomes apparent that many attributes of "psi" phenomena overlap. It has long been a contention of the serious parapsychologist that each of these types of phenomena is but a single manifestation of the same energy, force or function of an unconscious personality.

For example, when the Holland sensitive, van Delzen, touched the photograph of the missing brother-in-law and told the anxious relative that the man was still alive, clairvoyance, psychometry, precognition, and telepathy were all being manifested.

It is interesting to note how many "psi" activities are experienced while the percipient is either asleep or in the sleep-like states of trance or hypnosis. This may indicate that each of us, in our subconscious, has the faculties necessary to focus on the consciously unperceived world of ESP. Everyone who remembers his dreams has first-hand proof that there are various levels of mind. There is the one level that authors the "script" for the night's performance; another level which directs the play and cloaks it in the symbolism which psychiatrists tell us is necessary to sustain sanity; and there is yet another level that acts as the surprised captive audience for the performance. Continued research with dreams, such as the experiments currently being conducted by Drs. Montague Ullman and Stanley Krippner at Maimonides Hospital in Brooklyn, New York (which we shall examine in detail in Chapter Fourteen) may shed a new light on the powers that are man's very own.

In the literature of "psi" phenomena many clairvoyant experiences have been found to take place in dreams or while the percipient is in a relaxed state.

In 1949, Dorcie Calhoun who lived on a worn-out farm near Renovo, Pennsylvania, kept experiencing a persistent dream that told him there was natural gas underlying the nearby hills on his farm. Moreover, the dream kept showing him where to dig and urged him to take immediate action. At last the farmer managed to convince a number of local people to organize a small company and to begin drilling. Skeptics were stunned when the resulting well blew its top and required four days before experts could control the pillar of fire.

By 1951, there were nearly a hundred wells in the Renovo area, comprising the largest gas field in Pennsylvania. Original investors have seen their shares increase by 3,000 per cent, the little town of 3,000 citizens has doubled in size, and Dorcie Calhoun has become a wealthy man—all because of a dream.

Dr. Jan Ehrenwald has expressed his theory that telepathy is another "psi" phenomenon that works best when either the agent or the percipient is in what he labels a "state of psychological inadequacy." According to Dr. Ehrenwald, telepathy functions most effectively when the conscious mind is groggy with sleep, befogged by hypnosis, trance, fever, or physical exhaustion. In many cases, a brain defect or a glandular imbalance of some kind may increase telepathic prowess and accelerate other "psi" activity.

It should perhaps be clarified, before going much further into the world of ESP, that parapsychology is in no way synonymous with Spiritualism. To the uninformed layman, the psychical researcher is often thought of as some gullible man or woman who goes to seances to converse with the spirit of his late Uncle Henry. To be certain, mediums and their paranormal abilities are studied in all earnestness and seriousness in the laboratory. But these investigations are conducted under the most rigid scientific specifications, and there is no blind acceptance made of the allegedly spiritistic evidence produced by the mediums. Most often, quite the opposite is true.

A number of mediums, however, have successfully passed the rigorous tests of parapsychological laboratories and have proved to the satisfaction of the skeptical researcher that they were able to produce mental effects and materializations that lie beyond the ken of contemporary science. There can be little doubt that some of these men and women are marvelously gifted sensitives possessed of extraordinary powers of ESP. The lives of some of these individuals are dealt with in the chapter on mediumship along with the problem of survival evidence, which, if established, would definitely prove that non-physical man does survive after death.

Most parapsychologists believe that the difference between the genuine medium and the great majority of mankind lies in the fact that the sensitive's threshold of consciousness is set lower than that of others. In other words, the psychic sensitive has access to levels of awareness that lie beyond normal reach in the subconscious.

The spirit medium usually works in trance. While in this state of unconsciousness, the medium claims to be under the direction of a spirit guide or control. Spiritists believe in the reality of the guide as a spiritual entity apart from the medium. Parapsychologists hold that the control personality is but a secondary personality of the medium, that is able to dip into the powers of "psi" residing in the subconscious.

The physical phenomena of mediumship are among the most weird and dramatic of all occurrences studied by parapsychologists. Under laboratory conditions, mediums have produced materializations of human heads, hands, and even complete bodies from ectoplasm, a cloudy substance that seems to emanate from the medium's body. They have levitated themselves into the air, manifested stigmata on their bodies, caused mysterious apports (arrivals) of flowers, medallions, and items of clothing.

Some of the world's best minds have been vitally concerned with "psi" research. The British statesman William E. Gladstone, who, most of his life, was an avowed skeptic of paranormal occurrences, finally concluded that "psychical research is the most important work in the world today—by far the most important."

The famous statesman was not alone in his outspoken acclamation of the importance of "psi" research. Pierre Curie, who with his wife, Marie, discovered radium, stated, shortly before his death that in his opinion psychical research had more importance than any other. Freud belonged to both the English and the American societies for psychical research and said that he wished he had devoted more time to such study when he was younger. Carl Jung remained actively interested in "psi" experiments until his death.

Sir Arthur Conan Doyle, creator of Sherlock Holmes, became so obsessed with psychical research that he "killed off" his famous fictional character in order to devote full time to the Society for Psychical Research. The poet Yeats was out-spoken in discussing his own paranormal experiences. Aldous Huxley wrote a number of books dealing with psychic phenomena and, late in his life, began to concentrate on ESP and the drug experience.

Sir William Crookes, the great physicist, conducted an exhaustive study of "psi" phenomena. The German philosopher, Schopenhauer, insisted that such phenomena were the most important aspects of human experience and that it was the obligation of every scientist to know more about them. Julian Huxley, the biologist; Sir James Jeans, the astronomer; Arnold Toynbee, the historian; Alfred North Whitehead, the philosopher—all concerned themselves with ESP research.

In spite of the attention of such commanding intellects and the painstaking research of such men as J. B. Rhine, G. N. M. Tyrrell and S. G. Soal, parapsychologists are still regarded by an uncomfortable section of the scientific community as being "spook chasers," "crackpots," and as outright rebels and heretics to the bodies of established knowledge.

The basic reason for such disdain on the part of orthodox scientists is essentially the understandable reluctance of the scientific establishment to grant a hearing to a body of knowledge which might very well reshape or antiquate many of the premises on which its entire structure is based.

Arthur Koestler, noted novelist and journalist, tells of

his visit with a leading mathematical logician and philosopher. Koestler expressed his interest in recent statistical work in parapsychology. The logician loudly scoffed at such studies. Koestler, irritated by the man's closed mind, insisted that the statistics seemed sound.

"But who," the logician asked with a superior smile, "checked these statistics?"

Koestler named a world-famous statistician.

Upon hearing the man's name, the logician seemed completely nonplussed. After a few moments he said: "If that is true, it is terrible, terrible. It would mean that I would have to scrap everything and start from the beginning."

Orthodox scientists are not about to "scrap everything," and many of them feel that the best method of avoiding the research statistics compiled by parapsychologists is to insist upon the requirements demanded of all conventional sciences: (1) that they produce controlled and repeatable experiments, (2) that they develop a hypothesis comprehensive enough to include all "psi" activity from telepathy to poltergeists, from water dowsing to materializations.

The enormous difficulty in fulfilling these requirements can be immediately grasped by anyone with the slightest knowledge of "psi" phenomena. It would be impossible, for example, to repeat the apparition of a man's father as it appeared to him at the moment of his father's death. This sort of crisis apparition occurs only at death, and the man's father is going to die only once. "Psi" phenomena is almost completely spontaneous in nature, and ungovernable elements of mood and emotion obviously play enormously important roles in any type of paranormal experience. As G. N. M. Tyrrell wrote, a percipient is never aware of a telepathic, clairvoyant, or precognitive process at work within him. He is only aware of the *product* of that process. In fact, it seems apparent from laboratory work that conscious effort at determining any "psi" process at work within oneself will either completely destroy it or greatly diminish its effectiveness.

Therefore, laboratory experiments have sometimes established, by incredibly laborious tests and veritable mountains of statistics, only slightly better-than-chance evidence of the validity of telepathy, clairvoyance, precognition, and telekinesis. No one has yet managed to reproduce an apparition in a laboratory, and it is remarkable that the most gifted telepathic sensitive can have enough psychic energy to survive an endless series of card-guessing experiments.

"Psi" phenomena depends upon emotion and spontaneity for its most effective functioning. What is more sterile and emotionless than a laboratory? And what would serve to kill spontaneity more than a series of exceedingly boring laboratory tests? One researcher, allowing his frustration to be vented, complained about the absurdity of inhibiting the spontaneous feature of "psi" in order to maintain the control. "It would make as much sense to shoot an animal in order to study its habits," he sighed.

Science cannot afford to become dogmatic. Each generation seems to forget that scientists have had to admit some seemingly impossible facts in the past. Electricity, for example, was unknown except through a few sporadic events completely devoid of explanation, such as lightning and the mysterious attraction of bits of paper to rubbed amber. As facts became gradually accumulated, the theory of an electromagnetic field pervading all space was evolved.

Dr. Philip M. Morse, writing in the July, 1950, issue of *American Scientist,* said: "Almost immediately difficulties arose in trying to fit electromagnetic theory into classical mechanics. It was as though the two conceptual approaches, the preoccupation with matter, with forces incidental, and the preoccupation with a field of force, with matter incidental, were incompatible. One or the other would have to give way. What gave way was classical mechanics."

What gives way when "psi" is eventually accepted is not known. Perhaps, as many researchers believe, ESP will gradually merge with present day physics. Although at the present time "psi" phenomena seem to often contradict known physical laws, parapsychologists believe that the so-called paranormal will some day be seen to fit into the total scheme of nature.

But "psi" researchers are weary of being treated like second-class scientists. They insist that science must no longer ignore that which is not directly perceivable. In the field of *meson physics,* still largely unexplored, effect has been noted to have been followed by its cause. Perhaps precognition will cease to be considered odd to the physicist as he learns more about meson physics. Continued experiments in atomic physics may greatly illumine the mechanics of phenomena judged too impossible to comprehend today.

The world of ESP is a world of many strange and seemingly bizarre turns. In his *Psychic Science and Survival,* Hereward Carrington, a lifelong "psi" investigator, listed the following requirements of an ideal researcher: (1) a thorough knowledge of the literature of the subject; (2) a good grounding in normal and abnormal psychology, in physics, chemistry, biology, and photography; (3) keen powers of observation and an ability to judge human nature and its motives; (4) training in magic and sleight of hand; (5) shrewdness, quickness of thought and action, patience, resourcefulness, sympathy, and a sense of humor; (6) freedom from superstition; (7) the strength to stand out against bigotry, scientific as well as theological.

Do not deny yourself the excitement of further exploration in the world of ESP if you should feel deficient in one or more of Carrington's seven qualities. If you have that rarest of treasures, an open and unprejudiced mind, it will more than compensate for any other presumed shortcoming.

2.

ESP, PSYCHIATRY, AND THE
ANALYST'S COUCH

In 1884, the French psychiatrist, Pierre Janet, successfully conducted a most remarkable experiment in telepathy.

In 16 out of 25 tries, Janet telepathically hypnotized a young Frenchwoman, who sat in a room 500 meters away. Not only did the young woman enter the hypnotic state, but she obeyed Janet's post-hypnotic suggestions, which had been telepathically implanted in her subconscious.

The impressive experiment was observed by a group of scientists and presided over by the eminent French physician, Jean Martin Charcot. Janet later reported that they had taken "every plausible precaution . . . We can conclude only one thing: that such phenomena should be reproduced and studied."

Certainly Sigmund Freud (who may possibly have been an observer of the experiment since he was studying in Paris under Charcot at the time) would have given hearty recommendation in his later years to all psychoanalysts who wanted to devote time to the study of ESP. But such has not been the case. Although psychiatrists often give token approval of the work of "psi" research, there are perhaps less than ten in the entire United States who are actively engaged in any investigation of ESP. As a matter of rather dismal fact, there are only about six full-time and about 40 part-time academically trained "psi" researchers in America—and this number includes those few psychiatrists.

Dr. Jule Eisenbud, commenting upon the lack of psychiatric contributions to parapsychology in view of the potential which "psi" research could offer in the development of a comprehensive view of man's personality, recently wrote: ". . . there is every reason to be suspicious of a field of study which takes seriously a group of alleged phenomena and a set of propositions which correspond closely to delusions that always have characterized the mentally ill . . . which invariably disappear as the mentally disturbed regain the capacities, the balance, and relationships with people that are generally accepted as normal conditions of mental health."

As we have already mentioned, Freud, founder of psychoanalysis, would not have allowed possible censure from the scientific establishment to have thwarted his explorations into the unknown world of "psi" research. In the famous letter to the American researcher Hereward Carrington, Freud declared: "If I had my life to live over again, I should devote myself to psychical research rather than to psychoanalysis."

In his *The Psychopathology of Everyday Life* (1904), Freud had discussed several alleged super-normal occurrences and expressed a profound skepticism about prophetic dreams and telepathic phenomena. However, in 1922, he published his article "Dreams and Telepathy" and publicly proclaimed that he admitted the possibility of telepathic phenomena. He had written a much less cautious full-length essay, *Psychoanalysis and Telepathy,* which he would have read to the International Psychoanalytic Congress of 1922 if Ernest Jones had not persuaded him to consider the damaging repercussions his out-spoken attitude might have on the whole fledgling psychoanalytic movement. *Psychoanalysis and Telepathy,* consequently, did not see print until after Freud's death in 1941.

What had happened to so dramatically change Freud's

mind? Certainly two of his most brilliant friends and followers, C. G. Jung and Sandor Ferenczi, had much to do
with Freud's reappraisal of "psi" phenomena. Jung, who
later broke away from Freud to lead the "Jungian"
school of psychoanalysis, used to regale his friend and
mentor with tales of his own experiences in what the
Germans still often refer to as "occult" research. One
night, according to Freud's biographer, Ernest Jones,
Jung demonstrated his own ability as a poltergeist to the
astonished "father" of psychoanalysis. The hour was
late, and whether through power of mind or through the
influence of his powerful personality, Jung demonstrated
his ability to make objects rattle on the furniture in
Freud's study.

Ferenczi introduced Freud to several patients who
claimed to be clairvoyant. Freud was so struck by pre-
sumptive extrasensory communications between the analyst and his patients that he stated that the demonstrations had "put an end to any possible doubt about the
reality of thought-transference."

In 1924, Freud wrote a letter to Jones in which he
remarked how strongly he had been impressed with a
report on telepathic experiments which Gilbert Murray had prepared for the Society for Psychical Research.
"I confess," he wrote, ". . . that I am ready to give
up my opposition to the existence of thought-transference . . . I should even be prepared to lend the support of
psychoanalysis to the matter of telepathy."

Once again, the skeptic Jones, fearful of the damage
that such a public declaration might deliver to psychoanalysis, convinced Freud not to publish any such offer
of support to parapsychological research.

Today psychiatrists and psychoanalysts vary greatly in
their attitudes toward "psi" research. Those who profess
nothing but an adamant skepticism say that the illustrations of ESP brought forward by their colleagues express
nothing but the analyst's own desire to believe in their
validity. Those who consider "psi" research to be a seri-

ous and valuable contribution to man's understanding of his own personality insist that paranormal activities, particularly those of telepathy and clairvoyance, are too numerous to be dismissed by an arched eyebrow and a cursory examination.

Many psychiatrists have developed a respect for "psi" research when, during the course of analysis, a close relationship that can only be described as psychic, has developed between a doctor and his patient. Some doctors have reported patients who have related dreams that have dramatized actual incidents which the analysts themselves have experienced that day or even the week before. In several cases, the key to a patient's mental disturbance has been located in a dream experience of the analyst. Reports have even been made of several patients of the same analyst sharing dreams or re-enacting group or individual experiences, as if some strange circle of telepathic dreams had been established.

Dr. Jule Eisenbud has said that the "psi" process should be used in analysis. "The psi process is a thoroughgoing part of the total behavior of the individual and as much of a determinant in the actions and thoughts of the patient as other types of stimuli."

Commenting on "psi" during therapy, Dr. S. David Kahn, a New York psychiatrist, has written that ESP can often bring to the surface material which patients and analysts have repressed.

Dr. Montague Ullman says that "many persons who are incapable of effective communication in normal ways can communicate at a telepathic level and surprise the therapist with a telepathic dream of rich awareness even of the physician's problems.

"The telepathic dreams reported by patients in analysis are at times striking and often ingeniously linked to the dynamics of the treatment situation. But the occurrence of the dream is episodic and uncontrollable. It appears under conditions in which no advance preparation is made to exclude sensory cues."

It would seem obvious that since so much of Freudian theory and practice has to do with the interpretation of the symbols created during the dream experience the bonds between psychology and parapsychology are strong indeed. The same laws of psychodynamics that apply to the dream also apply to "psi" phenomena. Both the dream and "psi" are incompatible with currently accepted notions of time, space, and causality.

In 1928 Mr. Calder, who resided with his wife and family in Middlesex, was named headmaster of the Holmfirth Secondary School in Yorkshire, England.

Mrs. Calder had never been to Yorkshire, but shortly before they left Middlesex to begin househunting there, she had a vivid dream of an old greystone house located in a picturesque valley through which ran a stream of clear but strangely black-looking water.

No one was more startled than she when they found the very house of her dream in a valley near Holmfirth. The stream, which ran by the house, was often discolored by indigo from a nearby dye-works. The Calders decided to rent one-half of the large house, and they moved in during August, 1928.

The Calders often remarked about the strange dream that Mrs. Calder had experienced and were amazed at its clarity on all but one point. In her dream, Mrs. Calder had seen only that one half of the house which was already occupied. Outside of the door was half a barrel which was being used as a dog house. Although the other half of the house was occupied when the Calders moved in, there was no converted barrel dog house outside of its door.

About a year later, however, there was a change of tenants in the other half of the old greystone house in the valley. When the new tenants arrived, they brought with them a dog and set half a barrel outside the door for its kennel.

This precognitive dream, discussed in both H. F. Saltmarsh's *Foreknowledge* and Mrs. Alfred Lyttelton's

Some Cases of Prediction, seems indeed to do peculiar things to the popular concept of time. The fact that such precognitive dreams as those that tell of future events, accomplishments, dangers, and deaths are so common has persuaded many "psi" researchers that somehow, in a way that is not yet understood, each of us is aware of the future at an unconscious level of our minds. Such knowledge usually lies imprisoned at a subconscious level, out of the grasp of our conscious minds. Occasionally, however, in especially dramatic dreams, bits and snatches of scenes from the future bubble up to become conscious memories. Then, later, as the experience is lived through in waking reality, it is astonishing to have the dream play itself again before conscious eyes.

Psychiatrist Dr. Jan Ehrenwald has theorized that at the lower level of the subconscious—which Freudian analysts refer to as the "id"—time and spatial relationships may be all mixed up. Here and there, past, present, and future may all be interlocked and interchangeable.

The problems that await teams of psychiatrists and parapsychologists working together in joint efforts are many and varied, but each question answered brings us that much closer to a unified picture of man's personality and his role in the universal scheme of things.

For example, what about the trance state? In what ways is it similar to, or distinguished from, normal sleep, religious ecstasy, or hypnotically or drug induced states of unconsciousness?

What about mediumship? Does the medium serve as a receiving station for the unconscious patterns of others? Or is he in an altered state of personality, perhaps even possessed by a discarnate mind? And are the medium's spirit controls secondary personalities, or entities created by the mass mind of the seance circle?

And then there is multiple personality with sometimes three, four, or five faces of some hapless "Eve." Could it be, as some researchers have boldly suggested, that the human psyche, in a parthenogenetic fashion similar to the division of cells, may give birth to another "self"? Could this literal "split" of the personality become dissociated from the original self and, scornful of the accepted dimensions of time and space, become a poltergeist?

Psychiatrists have assured us that the various "personalities" involved in extreme cases of multiple personality may operate independently of one another and may carry out activities exclusive of the conscious awareness of any of the other personalities. One personality may, in fact, perform a function which another "face" would be loathe to do under any circumstances. In such cases there are, for all practical purposes, two or more "people" living in one body.

The problems in "psi" research proliferate and desperately call for a united frontal attack by a strong alliance of psychiatrists, psychoanalysts, and parapsychologists.

An example of the co-operation of a doctor and a sensitive in diagnosing obscure neuroses is Dr. R. C. Connell of County Cork, Ireland, and the psychometrist, Geraldine Cummins.

During the reign of terror effected against the Jews by the Nazis during World War II, a young Jew in his twenties came to Dr. Connell complaining of severe pains in his hands. After a brief examination, the doctor was able to determine a slight abrasion of skin and a minor injury to the extensor tendon of the little finger on one hand, but there was no fracture and absolutely no serious damage done.

Still the young man complained that both hands pained him so severely that he could not sleep at night. Dr. Connell assured him that complete recovery would be accomplished in a matter of days, but the man would not accept this diagnosis. Even a display of the X-ray plate could not convince him that his hands were not severely damaged. Dr. Connell at last concluded that the alleged pain caused by such a trivial injury was simply a mask to cover a more severe psychological trauma.

The young man freely related the way in which he had received the injury to his hand. Having lost his position as a branch manager of a large importing firm because of the war, he had taken employment as a fireman in the Belfast Fire Brigade. One day while saluting an officer, he had brought his hand down sharply on a fire pump that stood behind him. He was told by the hospital that the hand had received no serious injury, but he had not believed them and had come home to County Cork to undergo treatment at the hands of Dr. Connell.

The doctor could find no clues to the man's trauma in several extended discussions and at last proposed that they employ the services of Miss Geraldine Cummins, a psychiatrist, or object-reader. The young man consented and the doctor mailed Miss Cummins one of his fountain pens.

The sensitive, in a written report to Dr. Connell, said that the young Jew's difficulty lay in a brutal act which had been dealt to one of his ancestors over 100 years before, when a young Jewish husband had his hands cut off in punishment for defending his wife against the advances of a Russian landlord. The powerful landlord had organized a pogram that fired the Ghetto, drove out the Jews, and killed all members of the family except the young son. This son carried with him the terrible memory of a mutilated father, a ravished mother, and a slaughtered family.

The descendents of this emotionally scarred boy eventually made their way to County Cork, but the memory of the sadistic hacking-off of the hands lay buried in the subconscious of each of them.

When he was very young, the man who came to Dr. Connell with his injured hands had seen a close friend receive a severe cut on the hand. The horror of that wound began to free the terrible memory from his unconscious. Later a young man, who lived near them in the small Jewish community, scratched his hand and died of tetanus. This tragedy served to further reactivate the memory of the severed hands. When the Nazis began their systematic annihilation of the European Jews, the young man experienced the terrible fear and sorrow known to Jews everywhere during those grim and ghastly years of World War II. His taking of the job with the fire brigade intensified his subconscious recollection of the burning of the Ghetto, and when he injured his own hand, the psychological climax had been precipitated.

When Dr. Connell received this report from Miss Cummins, he called the young Jew to his office and read it to him.

"It's like I have heard it all somewhere, somehow, before," the young man told the doctor.

After a brief discussion, the young Jew indicated his conviction that Miss Cummins had indeed revealed the deep-seated psychological basis for his trauma. Incredible as it seemed, the true cause of the pain in his hands lay in the subconscious memory of a cruelty over 100 years old.

Dr. Connell adds that the young man recovered the complete control of his hands with astonishing rapidity and called on him later to announce his marriage plans. The combined efforts of a doctor and a psychic sensitive had utilized unorthodox channels of mind to effect a complete recovery in a psychologically disturbed young man.

3.

FORESEEING THE FUTURE

In her book, *Hidden Channels of the Mind,* Louisa E. Rhine, wife of world famous "psi" researcher, Dr. J. B. Rhine of Duke University, tells of a Maine man who reacted to a precognitive dream in the same way any normal well-adjusted twentieth century man might—he disregarded it. His rejection of the psychic warning may have cost his son's life.

The central figure in the case is nameless in Mrs. Rhine's book, but his personal data is on record in the files of the parapsychology laboratory at Duke University. The man's 14-year-old son, Walter, was an excellent swimmer, who often went swimming in a nearby stream with his neighborhood friends. In a dream, the man saw his son swimming below a certain big tree above the dam and drown. When he arrived at the stream, Walter's body had not yet been located, but a man named John McC—— was attempting to reclaim it from the water.

When the man awakened troubled and upset, his wife calmed him by saying that dreams never come true. In order not to tempt fate, however, she suggested that they not allow the boy to go swimming next day.

In the morning, the father dismissed it all as a silly dream and quickly began to busy himself with the routine details of running his store. When Walter came in later to tell his father that he was going to go swimming, the man was too preoccupied to even think of the dream.

Within a tragically short period of time, an excited

friend ran into the store and told the man that he had better get down to the stream in a hurry. Walter had been diving and had not come up. When the father arrived at the swimming hole, he had a sickening realization that the scene and the circumstances were exactly as they had been in his dream. The body had not yet been found, but John McC—— was diving for it. The father's sorrow was accentuated by the knowledge that his son's life might have been saved if he had heeded the warning that had come to him in his dream.

Is it possible to avoid forseen danger? "The answer," Mrs. Rhine writes, "is especially important to anyone who has had an experience that could be a preview of a coming catastrophe. If the impression is a genuine instance of precognition, must the calamity occur no matter what he does?"

The question is probably as old as man. Can man change the course of future events or is everything inexorably preordained? It is perhaps not so much a question of man's free will as it is a matter of what constitutes time.

"In any attempt to bridge the domains of experience belonging to the spiritual and physical sides of our nature," wrote A. S. Eddington, "Time occupies the key position."

What is time? Precognitions have been noted regularly not only in the literature of psychical research but in that of science itself for more than 2,000 years. The Bible includes a remarkable collection of divinely inspired prophecies and promises. Throughout the several centuries of cerebral man's existence, a large and impressive argument has been building up which declares man's conception of time as an absolute to be a naive one. A great number of recent "psi" researchers have speculated that the common concept of time might be due to the special pattern in which man's sensory apparatus has evolved. It seems evident from the marked occurrences of precognitive dreams that some people do occasionally break loose from the evolved sensory pattern to receive a glimpse of the true order of the universe.

Mark Twain (Samuel L. Clemens) was one of these people. When he was a young man, he had a dream that his handsome brother, Henry, who served on the same Mississippi River steamboat as he did, would be killed.

In the dream, he saw his brother lying in a metal casket. On his breast lay a spray of white flowers with one red rose at its center. In the morning, Clemens told his sister of the eerie dream, then decided to put it off as "just one of those strange things."

When he returned to the steamboat, *Pennsylvania,* he learned that he had been transferred to the *A. T. Lacey.* He bade his brother good-bye and they made plans to meet in Memphis. The *Pennsylvania* was pulling out that day. The *A. T. Lacey* would not follow for another two days.

By the time Clemens' steamship pulled into Memphis, the *Pennsylvania* was only a violent memory of a terrible explosion that the citizens of Memphis discussed in excited spurts of conversation. To his horror, Clemens learned that his brother's ship had burst into flame just as it approached Memphis. He finally located his brother, who, critically wounded, had been taken to a hastily improvised hospital. For four days and nights, Clemens was seldom away from his injured brother's bedside. The sorrowful vigil ended only when Henry died.

Exhausted after four sleepless nights, Clemens went to his boarding house to rest before attending to his brother in the mortuary. When he arrived at the funeral parlor, the establishment was filled with the bodies of other victims of the *Pennsylvania* disaster. Henry's body was the only one that had been placed in a metal casket. The casket, Clemens was told, was a gift from the ladies of Memphis, who had been impressed by Henry's youth and unusual handsomeness. As the tearful Sam stood looking down at his brother, a lady stepped up to the casket and laid a bouquet of white flowers, with a single red rose at its center, on Henry's chest.

One thing seems certain about true precognition: whether it comes about through a dream or the vision of a seer, the percipient does not see *possibilities* but *actualities*.

In view of this, some researchers maintain that the age-old query, "Can the future be changed?" has no meaning. The foreknowledge of the future, of which some level of the subconscious is aware and of which it sometimes flashes a dramatic bit or scene to the conscious in a dream or trance, is founded on the knowledge of how the individual will use his freedom of choice. The "future event" conditions the subconscious self. The level of the subconscious that "knows" the future does not condition the "future event." The transcendent element of self which knows what "will be" blends all time into "what is now and what will always be." For the conscious self, what is now the past was once the future. We do not look upon past events and feel that we acted without freedom of will. Why then should we look at the future and feel that those events are predetermined? That a subconscious level in the psyche may *know* the future, these researchers insist, does not mean that the conscious self has no freedom of choice. Simply stated, if the future could be changed it would not be the future. In a true precognitive experience when one perceives the future, he has glimpsed what will be and what, for a level of subconscious, already exists.

On a July morning in 1952, according to a case in the files of Louisa E. Rhine, a woman in New Jersey attempted to avoid the death of a child as she had foreseen it in a precognitive "vision."

In this glimpse of the future, which had occurred as she lay resting in a darkened room, she envisioned the aftermath of a dreadful traffic accident. A child had been killed and lay covered on the ground. Because the child was covered, the woman could not identify the victim.

In the morning, she told her next-door neighbor of the strange dream and begged her to keep close watch on her five-year-old child. Next she phoned a son, who lived in a busy section of the town, and admonished him to keep an eye on his two small children. She had another son who lived in the country, but she felt there was little need to warn him to be wary of traffic. Nonetheless, it was his little Kathy who was killed that same day when a township truck backed into her.

There are, perhaps, five types of precognitive experiences. At the most elementary level is subliminal precognition, or the 'hunch' that proves to be an accurate one. There is no slur intended in labeling this type of experience elementary. Some hunches—as we shall see a bit later—have saved lives. Next would come trivial precognition, which takes place only a short time before the actual occurrence of a rather unimportant event. Then, in the area of full-blown, meaningful precognitions, which indicate a power of mind not limited by space or time, there are beneficial, non-beneficial, and detrimental pre-visions.

In a beneficial premonition, the transcendent self may over-dramatize a future event in such a way that it proves to be a warning which is acted upon by the conscious self's characteristic reaction to such a crisis.

To take a final example from Mrs. Rhine: A young mother in Washington State awakened her husband one night and related a horrible dream. She had seen the large ornamental chandelier that hung above their baby's crib, crash down into the child's bed and crush the infant to death. In the dream, as they ran to discover the terrible accident, she noticed that the hands of the clock on the baby's dresser were at 4:35.

The man laughed at his wife's story, rolled over, and went back to sleep. Although she felt foolish for doing so, the young woman slid out of bed, went into the nursery, and returned with the baby. Placing the sleeping child gently between them, the woman fell at once into a deep sleep.

A few hours later, the young couple were awakened by a loud, crashing noise. The sound had come from the nursery, and the couple found that the chandelier had fallen into the baby's crib. The clock on the baby's dresser indicated the time as 4:35.

For the young woman's deep level of subconscious, the falling of the chandelier was a *present* fact that was still a *future* fact for her conscious self. The absence of the baby in its crib was also a present fact to the transcendental self because it was aware of how the conscious self of the young mother would react if she knew the safety of her child was threatened. To stimulate the woman to action, the deep level of her psyche formulated a dramatic precognitive dream with an attached tragic ending. The future, therefore, had not been altered by the woman's action, only implemented.

Volume L, Number 3 of the *Journal* of the American Society for Psychical Research carries a fascinating account of statistical research conducted by William E. Cox, which seems to indicate that subconscious forewarnings (or "hunches") may keep people off accident-bound trains.

Cox selected passenger trains for his study for two basic reasons. First, the passenger-carrying capacities of airplanes, ships and busses is fixed, while a train can add or remove cars as the traffic demands. Second, subways and busses do not keep the kind of accurate records of passenger traffic that would be required for such a narrow statistical study as the one Cox was about to conduct. To prove his hypothesis, Cox needed to obtain both the total number of passengers on the train at the time of the accident and the total number of passengers on the same train during each of the preceding seven days, and on the 14th, 21st, and 28th day before the accident.

Cox compiled separate statistics for Pullman passengers. He reasoned, quite logically it seems, that, as Pullman passengers had usually reserved their space on the train sometime in advance, they would be less likely to give credence to a subliminal precognition or a hunch that they should not carry out plans made previously. Also, someone who has established a thought-pattern of a business or pleasure trip and has been contemplating the activity for a number of days would probably have a mind that was hyperactive rather than in the relaxed state so conducive to "psi" phenomena.

The statistical tables compiled by Cox demonstrated the astonishing evidence that passengers did avoid accident-bound trains. In a study that concerned eleven train accidents, seven of the eleven carried fewer coach passengers than they had carried on the previous day; six carried fewer passengers than they had the same day on the preceding week, and four carried the lightest loads of the eight-day period.

In an investigation of seventeen accidents involving Pullman passengers, ten of the trains carried fewer passengers than they had on the same day of the previous week. Five carried the lightest load of the eight-day period. Cox later extended his research to include thirty-five accidents, and found that his data applied to eighty per cent of the cases. With the final results of Cox's figures, the odds are better than 100 to 1 that some form of "psi" was involved rather than pure chance.

Cases of detrimental precognition are interesting to analyze, because in these instances, the act of fore-seeing seems almost to have helped to produce the unfortunate result.

A graphic example of detrimental precognition would be the dream that occurred to Ralph Lowe on the night before his horse, *Gallant Man*, was to run in the 1957 Kentucky Derby.

Gallant Man, an odds-on favorite to win, had the added advantage of being ridden by Willie Shoemaker, one of the top jockeys in the United States. Mr. Lowe, therefore, could not be blamed when he awoke in anger and consternation at what he had witnessed in his dream. He had "seen" *Gallant Man* leading the pack coming down the home stretch. It appeared to be an easy victory for the Derby favorite. Then, inexplicably, Willie Shoemaker pulled up and allowed another horse to cross the finish line ahead of *Gallant Man*.

That morning before the race, the disturbing dream still adding to his already nervous state of mind, Lowe told Shoemaker, "Don't pull him up short, Willie!"

The jockey frowned at the owner's peculiar admonition. Why would Lowe say such a thing? No jockey in the history of the Kentucky Derby had ever pulled a horse up short of the finish line.

That afternoon, when the race was run, an incredulous crowd at the Derby saw Willie Shoemaker mistake the 16th pole for the finish line and pull up *Gallant Man*. *Iron Liege* pounded by the horse that had had a comfortable lead coming into the home stretch and won by half a length.

Mr. Lowe's precognition had indeed been an accurate and certainly a detrimental one. If he had not planted the notion of pulling the horse up short in Willie Shoemaker's mind, the incident might never have occurred to the experienced jockey.

In 1934, H. F. Saltmarsh issued a report to the London Society for Psychical Research in which he had made a critical study of 349 cases of precognition. Saltmarsh established the following conditions which would, in his estimation, make a case of precognition wholly satisfactory:

(a) It should have been recorded in writing or told to a witness or acted upon in some significant manner *before* the subsequent incident verified it.

(b) It should contain a sufficient amount of detail verified by the event to make chance coincidence unlikely.

(c) Conditions should be such that we can definitely rule out the following as explanations: telepathy and contemporary clairvoyance, auto-suggestion, inference from subliminally acquired knowledge and hyperaesthesia.

Saltmarsh used these criteria to proclaim 183 of the 349 cases as being wholly satisfactory cases of precognition.

One of these, the "Case of the Derailed Engine," will serve as an illustration of the sort of experience that Saltmarsh deemed as truly precognitive.

A minister's wife and daughter were staying at lodgings at Trinity, near Edinburgh, Scotland, on July 15, 1860. It was a bright Sunday afternoon, and between three and four o'clock, Mrs. W. told her daughter to go out for a short walk on the railway garden—this was the name she had given a strip of ground between the seawall and the railway embankment.

The daughter had only been gone a few minutes when Mrs. W. distinctly heard a voice within her say: "Send for her back or something dreadful will happen to her."

Mrs. W. was seized by a sense of foreboding which progressed into a feeling of terror that soon had her trembling and physically upset over the nameless dread. She ordered a servant to go and bring her daughter home at once.

The servant, seeing her mistress visibly distraught, set out immediately. Mrs. W. paced the floor, more upset than ever, fearful that she would never again see her daughter alive.

In about a quarter of an hour, the servant returned with the daughter, who was safe and well. Mrs. W. asked the child not to play on the railroad embankment and obtained her promise that she would sit elsewhere and not on the spot where she usually played.

Later that afternoon an engine and tender jumped the rails and crashed into the wall where Miss W. had been playing before the servant brought her home. Three men out of five who were there, were killed. Much later, Miss W. and her brother visited the scene of the tragedy and saw that the smashed engine had crashed into the precise spot where she had spent two hours with her brother on the previous Sunday afternoon.

Saltmarsh theorized that what we call the "present moment" is not a point of time, but a small time interval called the "specious present." According to his theory, our subconscious minds have a much larger "specious present" that our conscious level of being. For the subconscious, all events would be "present." If, on occasion, some of this subconscious knowledge were to burst into the conscious, it would be interpreted as either a memory of a past event or a precognition of a future event. We know that the past is neatly cataloged somewhere in our subconscious. Some "psi" researchers, such as H. F. Saltmarsh, believe that all events—past, present, and future—are part of the "present" for the deeper transcendental mind.

In his book, *An Experiment with Time,* J. W. Dunne gives many examples of his own precognitive dreams, which he recorded over a period of several years. Dunne firmly believed in sleep and dreams as the prime openers of the subconscious and formulated a philosophy, which he called "Serialism," to account for precognition. In Dunne's view, time was an "Eternal Now." All events that have ever occurred, that exist now, or that ever will be, are everlastingly in existence. In man's ordinary, concious, waking state, his view is only of the present. In sleep, however, the individual's view might be sufficiently enlarged to allow several glimpses of the future. Although Dunne's theory is considered too deterministic by the majority of "psi" researchers and has been generally discredited, the philosophy of "Serialism," as advanced in *An Experiment with Time*, offers the challenge of bold and imaginative thinking.

One of Dunne's theories in relation to *déja vuè,* the sense of the already seen, is quite intriguing. Dunne suggests that this curious experience (which almost everyone has had at one time or another) of "having been here before," is due to the stimulation of a partially remembered precognitive dream. When the conversation becomes familiar or the new location becomes suddenly recognizable, one may, according to Dunne, simply be remembering a precognitive dream, which had been driven back into the subconscious.

Who has not known this strange feeling of having been with precisely *these* friends in *this* particular room and hearing exactly *this* dialogue at some former time? The fact that psychologists have chosen to call this uncanny sensation *déja vuè* has certainly done nothing to explain this eerie phenomenon.

Such a mystical sounding term would have meant little to explain things to Chauncey Depew, who was once a runner-up for the Republican Presidential nomination and who delivered the speech nominating Colonel Theodore Roosevelt as candidate for Governor of New York.

Depew's ringing oratory clinched the nomination for Roosevelt and set the dynamic "Teddy's" political career in motion. But who would have believed Depew if he had told anyone that he had lived through that political convention at some time in the past and had even delivered that identical speech? What is more, Depew remembered exactly when the "other time" had taken place, because he had taken notes throughout the entire experience.

He had been sitting on the porch of his country home on the Hudson just one week before the convention. Relaxed, gazing idly at the opposite shore, Depew was suddenly puzzled to see the pastoral landscape become transformed into Convention Hall. Blinking his eyes incredulously, Depew saw the delegates taking their seats, and heard a temporary chairman make the motion to proceed with the nominations. Then, Depew heard himself giving a rousing speech for Colonel Roosevelt. When he finished, the convention erupted into wild cheering, and Depew took his seat with a pleased smile as a triumphal march began around the hall.

At that point, the raucous political scene faded, and Depew once again found himself staring at the quiet Palisades across the Hudson. Although he was completely baffled by the strange phenomenon that he had just witnessed, Depew was not one to waste such a wonderful opportunity. Grabbing paper and pen, he quickly jotted down the speech he had just heard himself delivering. It was this same speech that he repeated with the same success a week later.

If man can glimpse the future in precognitive dreams, it also follows that certain sensitive people may have the ability to step into a scene of the past. Knowledge of some past event or state acquired through other than normal sensory channels or inference based on sensory data is termed *retrocognition.*

In August, 1901, two English ladies, both estimable scholars, Miss C. Anne E. Moberly, principal of St. Hugh's College, Oxford, and Eleanor F. Jourdain, a member of her staff, suddenly and quite inadvertently, found themselves in the Petit Trianon as it existed in the time of Marie Antoinette. Not at all a rigid tableau or fuzzy vision, the scene was completely "live" and featured several gardeners and villagers dressed in clothes of another era and speaking an archaic French. Buildings existed that were not on current maps, and there were no other tourists about. Each woman confessed later that she had felt oppressed and nervous during the strange incident. Their story was afterwards confirmed by documents in the French National Archives.

Mrs. Coleen Buterbaugh is employed as a secretary to Dr. Sam Dahl, Dean of Nebraska Wesleyan College in Lincoln. On October 23, 1963, at precisely 8:50 A.M., Mrs. Buterbaugh stepped into an office in the old C. C. White building on an errand for the Dean. As she stepped into the two-room suite, she noticed that both rooms were empty and the windows were open. But as she moved farther into the room, she had "the strangest feeling that I was not in the office alone.

"I looked up and just for what must have been a few seconds saw the figure of a woman standing with her back to me, at a cabinet in the second office. She was reaching up into one of the drawers."

Mrs. Buterbaugh had never seen the woman before that instant. The woman was tall, slender, dark-haired, and dressed in the style of an earlier time.

"I still felt that I was not alone," Mrs. Buterbaugh later told Rose Sipe of the Lincoln *Evening Journal*. "I felt the presence of a man sitting at the desk to my left, but as I turned around there was no one there.

"I gazed out the large window behind the desk and the scenery seemed to be that of many years ago. There were no streets. The new Willard sorority house that now stands across the lawn was not there. Nothing outside was modern. By then I was so frightened, that I turned and left the room!"

Mrs. Buterbaugh appeared so pale and shaken that Dean Dahl feared she was on the verge of a collapse. At last he got the story from her, and, together, they went to see Dr. Glenn Callen, chairman of the division of social sciences, who had been on the Nebraska Wesleyan faculty since 1900. There, with the help of Dr. Callen's memory and old college yearbooks, Mrs. Buterbaugh identified the apparition she had seen as being Miss Clara Mills, who had died in that office.

Somehow, Mrs. Buterbaugh had walked into Miss Mills' office as it had been in the 1920's. In a 1915 yearbook, a picture of Miss Mills bore the caption: "A daughter of the gods thou art, divinely tall and most divinely fair." The picture and the description matched the appearance of the tall, dark-haired woman Mrs. Buterbaugh had seen in the office.

"I'm not one to imagine things," Mrs. Buterbaugh affirmed. "But when I close my eyes, I can see her just as plain as day."

In 1916, Miss Edith Olivier was driving through a dreary October evening from Devizes to Swindon in Wiltshire, England. As she left the main road, she found herself passing along a strange avenue of huge gray megaliths, and she concluded that she must be approaching Avebury, which had originally been a circular megalithic temple approached by long stone avenues. Although she had never been to Avebury before, she had seen pictures of the area in archaeological texts.

When she arrived at the end of the avenue, she got out of the automobile and climbed on to the bank of a large earthwork. Here, she could view the irregularly fallen megaliths and the several cottages which had been constructed among them. On that particular night, in spite of the rain, a village fair seemed to be merrily in progress. Miss Olivier watched in amusement as she saw villagers walking about with flares and torches, enjoying the various booths and shows. If it had not been for the rain, which was becoming increasingly heavy, Miss Olivier would have watched the pleasant tableau longer.

When she visited Avebury again, some nine years later, she was puzzled to read in the guidebook that, although a village fair had once been an annual occurrence in Avebury, the custom had been abolished in 1850. In addition, she learned that the particular avenue of megaliths on which she had driven on her first visit had disappeared before 1800.

This kind of experience seems to lend a great deal of credence to the theory that a kind of persistent memory exists in the psychic ether associated with a particular place. Thomas A. Edison theorized that since no form of energy is ever lost, scenes of the past may become imprinted somewhere on this psychic ether just as images are registered on motion picture film. If this theory is established, it would explain such transgressions of the boundaries of the past, for a person of the proper sensitivity might be able to pick up the etheric images of past events in much the same manner as a projector runs a spool of film past a beam of light projecting an image of "life" on the screen.

An alternate theory is that surviving minds, emotionally held to the area, may telepathically invade the mind of the sensitive and enable him to see the scene as "they" once saw it. It cannot be denied that some places definitely have their own "atmospheres," which often give sensitive people feelings of uneasiness—if not downright discomfort and fear. Whether this may be caused by surviving minds, a psychic residue, or the impression of a persistent memory in the psychic ether is a question that will be discussed again in relation to the appearance of ghosts in "haunted houses."

Excellent examples of what seem to be impressions caused by the collective emotions and memories of large groups of people can be found in those cases where battle scenes of the past have been "refought" for reluctant witnesses.

The Phantom Battle of Edge Hill is more substantial than many such reports because its authenticity is substantiated by so many witnesses of good standing. The actual battle was fought near the village of Keinton, England, on October 23, 1642, between the Royalist Army of King Charles and the Parliamentary Army under the Earl of Essex.

On Christmas Eve, several country folk were awakened by the approaching sounds of drums, marching soldiers, and the boom of artillery pieces. Thinking that it could only be another clash between soldiers of the flesh, the people fled from their houses to confront two armies of ghosts. One side bore the king's colors; the other, Parliament's banners.

Until two or three in the morning, the phantom armies had at one another in a spectral "re-run" of the battle that had taken place two months before. There was the sharp crackle of muskets, the boom of cannon, the neighing of charging horses, the screams and cries of the dying. When the king's army fled as it had done before, the Parliamentary forces stood about cheering and giving thanks for their victory. Then, slowly, the scene of spectral carnage faded, and the hillsides were once again quiet in the hush of a Christmas Eve.

When the frightened countryfolk made their way to the village and to William Wood, justice of the peace, they were met with violent skepticism. Wood and Samuel Marshall, the village clergyman, scoffed at the story and tried to shame the folk for using Christmas Eve to concoct such a foolish and fanciful tale. In order to shake the witnesses—who stood fast by their tale—the two men agreed to accompany them to Edge Hill on the next night. There, in spite of their unwillingness to believe in such happenings, Justice Wood and Reverend Marshall saw the entire battle re-fought in its minutest detail. Repeat performances of the ghostly strife were held on the two following evenings as well.

At last the word reached the ears of King Charles at Oxford. The king was hardly pleased that a ridiculous fantasy conjured up by simple countryfolk should be keeping the memory of his defeat at Edge Hill before the entire English public. He made his desire to squelch such a superstitious tale quite clear to Colonel Louis Kirke, Captain Dudley, and Captain Wainman, whom he dispatched to Keinton to expose the whole impossible business.

The three officers were highly skeptical men, who never believed anything they could not perceive directly with their own five senses. They went to Reverend Marshall and belabored him for being a party to the circulation of such preposterous rumors. They threatened to have Justice Wood removed from office. They interviewed villagers and countryfolk and tried to trip them up in some badly told lie. Frustrated that everyone in the village of Kein-

ton and in the surrounding countryside stood adamant-
ly by the story of a phantom battle at Edge Hill, the officers were nonetheless in a gay and light-hearted mood
when they at last consented to sit out on the hillside on
Saturday and Sunday nights to witness the ghostly encounter for themselves.

Incredulously, the three emissaries of the king's disbelief observed the phantom battle on each night. In
addition to witnessing the incredible phenomenon, the
officers were able to recognize several of their fallen
comrades, particularly Sir Edmund Varney. When they
returned with their report to King Charles, all three
officers took an oath that their testimony was true.

Two young Englishwomen, sisters-in-law, were sharing a room on the second floor of a building where German troops had been quartered at Dieppe during World
War II. The time was August, 1951. Nine years previously, nearly 1,000 young Canadians had lost their lives
in the ill-fated Dieppe Raid.

On the morning of August 4th, the two vacationing
Englishwomen were awakened just before dawn by terrible sounds of guns and shell fire, dive bombing planes,
shouts, and the scraping of landing craft hitting the beach.
The frightening cacophony continued until the coming of
light and the sounds of normal activity. The women had,
of course, cautiously peered out of the windows and
stepped out on the balcony shortly after the nightmarish
memory of sound had begun, but at no time did they
ever see anything that would account for the simulated
invasion. Even more peculiarly, no one else in the house
was awakened or mentioned being disturbed by the
sounds.

The young Englishwomen were so impressed by the
ordeal, however, that they began to prepare a report to
send to the Society for Psychical Research. Being possessed of unusual presence of mind, they had added
much value to their report by keeping a record by their

watches of the precise time which the phenomena began
and the exact times of the ebb and flow of battle. S.
P.R. investigators checked the ladies' report against the
detailed accounts of the actual raid in the war office. The
times, as recorded by the women, were often identical
to the minute of the raid that had taken place nine years
before. In other instances, their times were off by only
a minute or two.

"Time," moaned a puzzled Saint Augustine, "what is
it? If nobody asks me, I know. But if I am asked, I do
not know!"

Obviously, the conventional idea of time existing as
some sort of stream flowing along in one dimension is
an inadequate one. In this view, the past does not exist:
it is gone forever. The future does not exist because it
has not yet happened. The only thing that exists is the
present moment. But wait! The present does not really
exist, either, since it is no sooner "now" than that "now"
becomes part of the past. What was the future when you
began to read this sentence is fleetingly the present and
has already become the past by the time you read the
next word.

If the past completely ceased to exist, we should have
no memory of it. Yet each of us has a large and varied
memory bank. Therefore, the past must exist in some
sense; not, of course, as a physical or material reality,
but in some sphere of its own. Similarly, certain researchers maintain, the future must also exist in some way in
a sphere of its own. The subconscious does not differen-
tiate between past, present, and future but is aware of all
spheres of time as part of the "Eternal Now."

There are certain kinds of precognitive experiences
that can be easily identified as part of the normal process
of the subconscious. A woman dreams of coming down
with the measles and laughs it off. She did not succumb
to the disease as a child, why should she weaken as an

adult? In two days, she is in bed with the annoying rash covering her body. Rather than judge this to be a prophetic dream, we might better regard the experience as an example of the subconscious mind being much more aware of the condition of the inner body than the superficial mind.

In other cases, a keen intellect and a great awareness of one's environment will enable one to make predictions. Much of the affluence our contemporary economy, from stock market juggling to hemline raising, is based upon the ability of certain knowledgeable people to make predictions concerning the preferences of a mass society.

In contrast to these "explainable" predictions, however, are the many examples of men and women who seem beyond any doubt to have experienced precognitions. This "power of prophecy" rested not in some occult knowledge, but within the transcendent self, which seems to be aware of events that belong in the realm of the future for the superficial self.

Some "psi" researchers have presented time in an analogy with a man riding on the rear platform of a train. The man looks to the left and to the right. As the train chugs along, he is able to see a panorama of new scenes as they come into his view. As the train continues, these scenes fade into the distance and are lost to view. They have become the man's past. But these scenes do continue to exist after they have passed from the man's view, and they were in existence before the man perceived them, even though he was only able to see them at the time that they were his present. However, if another man were flying high above the train in an airplane, he would be able to see the train passenger's past and present, as well as future scenes which lie beyond the man's limited ground-level view. All would exist for the man in the airplane as an "Eternal Now."

The problem of time will not be an easy one to solve.

In the words of philosopher Alfred North Whitehead: "It is impossible to meditate on Time and the mystery of the creative passage of Nature without an overwhelming emotion at the limitations of human intelligence."

4.

TELEPATHY, TWINS, AND TUNING
MENTAL RADIOS

At about 4:00 P.M. on July 1, 1951, Mrs. Frances Wall had just finished bathing and setting her hair and had lain down on the bed to read until her husband returned from an outing at the park.

She had begun to doze off when she suddenly heard her husband's voice cry out in anguish: "Frances, come to the park. I'm drowning!"

His voice was so loud and distinct that Mrs. Wall thought at first that it had come from the apartment. She sat up, stunned, trying to clear her head.

"Please, Frances, please hurry!"

Sickened by the sudden realization that something dreadful was happening to her husband, Mrs. Wall hurried to put on a robe and ran from the apartment. When she was halfway to the lake in the park, she could see a crowd gathering near the shore. She knew without going a step further that her husband had drowned.

On May 19, 1931, a nurse reported a similar telepathic crisis linkage for the *Journal* of the Society for Psychical Research.

Shortly before she was to go on night duty, Miss Margaret Jones was awakened by a voice calling: "Margaret, Margaret." She had a distinct impression that someone rushed into her room and back out again.

Puzzled, she got out of bed and looked down the corridor. There was no one in sight. Not being able to determine any reason for alarm, Miss Jones began to get dressed. It must have been a maid who had awakened her for duty, she thought. But she was still mystified, especially in view of the fact that no one at the hospital had ever called her by her first name.

When she finally looked at her clock, she saw that she had been awakened at 5:30 A.M. As the night nurses were not usually awakened until 7:30, Miss Jones sat down on her bed completely baffled.

Later, while she was on duty, Miss Jones received a telegram that informed her that her niece had passed away at 5:30 A.M. When she went to be with her sister in her sorrow, she learned that the child had suddenly taken ill, and although an immediate operation had been performed, she had only lived for a few hours. As she lay dying, the child had called out: "Margaret, Margaret."

These two cases bear out the contention that telepathy (and ESP in general) functions best between individuals who have a strong emotional link. This particular level of man's mind seems to operate best spontaneously, especially when a crisis situation makes it necessary to communicate through other than the standard sensory channels.

Parapsychologists have long been aware that twins show unusually high telepathic rapport. A series of tests conducted by psychologists at the University of Alberta, Canada, confirmed this theory by establishing statistical evidence that identical twins, and to a lesser extent, fraternal twins, have remarkable ability to communicate with one another through ESP.

At the behest of Dr. J. B. Rhine of Duke University, Mrs. Olivia Rivers, a psychologist at Mississippi State University, conducted tests with identical twins, Terry and Sherry Young. The pretty Jackson, Mississippi, twins were able to pass entire sentences to each other via telepathy. The girls seemed to be in constant rapport and even when separated, each knew if the other had turned

an ankle, got a toothache, or developed a cold. Sherry
was better as the receiver, Terry as the sender.

Their schoolteachers despaired of ever receiving an
accurate test from either girl. Even when placed in separate classrooms the girls still used similar phrases and
got similar marks. They made no secret of the fact
that they helped one another in their school work, but
insisted that it was by telepathy alone. It was not cheat-
ing to them, nor could anyone consider it as being
unfair or dishonest of the girls. It was not their fault
if their minds functioned as one.

In an article by Jhan and June Robbins, "Can Twins
Read Each Others' Minds?" which appeared in the January 28, 1962, issue of *This Week,* Dr. Robert Sommer
is quoted as saying: "Identical twins obviously share the
closest possible relationship that can embrace two human
beings. They actually started out as a single individual—
and they have the same mental and physical attributes."

Dr. Sommer and his associates studied several twins
whose ages ranged from 16 to 50. Their interviews dis-
closed that fully one-third of the twins had had "psi"
experiences with their "other halves."

Occasionally a strange case comes to light where twins
have separated at birth, grow up unaware that they even
have a twin, yet, when confronted with their "double"
several years later, are amazed that their lives have os-
tensibly followed one path.

The Tacoma, Washington, *News Tribune,* January 12,
1959, carried one such incredible story.

Margaret Judson, who grew up in Vancouver, was repeatedly baffled whenever, as a member of the Canadi-
an Women's Army Corps, she was sent to Toronto. Here
people persisted in calling her "Marion" and told her
that she had a double living in that city. After her term
of service, Margaret returned to Toronto, determined to
track down her alleged duplicate.

When "Margaret" at last faced "Marion" across the
counter of a department store, they were both wearing

similar brown suits. Startled at being confronted with their mirror-image, the women soon determined over 21 astonishing parallels in their lives. They had been born twins in Toronto in 1924 and put out for adoption. Neither had ever been told that she had a twin sister. In the same month that Margaret had joined the CWAC, Marion had tried to join up but had failed.

Both had been expert roller skaters in their teens. They had, in their geographically separated but psychically united lives, both taken piano lessons, sung alto in church choirs, had their tonsils removed in the same year. They had both married sailors who were the same age, size, weight, and build, who had been in the service four years, and had decided upon the navy as a career.

When they met in the department store, they had been wearing similar brown suits. As a weird capper, the next time that they met, both women wore identical plaid skirts and similar heart-shaped lockets, which had been gifts from their foster mothers on their 21st birthdays!

Daily newspapers repeatedly carry stories of twins who have received identical injuries at the same time. I once knew twin sisters who even bore identical skin blemishes as they progressed through puberty.

A Chicago telephone company employe, unaware that he had a twin, had been called "Fred" by strangers often enough to arouse his curiosity. His parents admitted that he had been an adopted son and had an identical twin. He found his twin in Topeka, Kansas where both men were astonished to learn that they were both employed by Bell Telephone, had married in the same year to girls of a similar nature and type. In addition to having received the same kind of education in homes of similar background and having married women of the same general type, each had a four-year-old son and a fox terrier named Trixie.

Experiments with twins are offering "psi" researchers their greatest proofs of telepathy. These astonishing demonstrations have done much to break down the intellectual resistance built up by many physical scientists and have opened the door for the tentative acceptance of other "psi" phenomena into the domain of accepted knowledge.

Remarkable experiments have also been conducted with primitive peoples to test the hypothesis that telepathy is an archaic means of communication, which, although remaining as a vestigial function of mind, was once the sole method for conveying ideas.

It has been observed that the primitive bushmen in Australia can accurately transmit thoughts, feelings, and ideas to friends and relatives several miles away. They also use "psi" abilities to locate missing objects, straying cattle, and thieving enemies. The bushmen live a Stone Age existence. Their normal sensory abilities have been heightened by their struggle for survival. Their eyes can identify objects at great distances without the aid of field glasses. Their powers of smell are probably on a par with that of a sensitive collie. Their ESP talents are even more remarkable.

Dr. A. P. Elkin, an anthropologist from Sydney University, was forced to re-arrange some of his scientific thinking after he had conducted some studies among the bushmen. In his *Aboriginal Men of High Degree,* Dr. Elkin writes that although his arrival was never announced by messenger, drums, or smoke signals, each village was prepared for his arrival, knew where he had just come from, and was aware of the purpose of his wilderness trek.

Whenever the anthropologist heard of a case where a native claimed to have gained personal information telepathically from a faraway village, subsequent investigation proved the knowledge to be accurate. Whether the information concerned a dying parent, the birth of a nephew, or the victory of a successful hunt, the recipients' knowledge of the event was completely in accordance with the actual happening.

Dr. Elkin was told: "Thoughts, though invisible, can be sent flying through the air."

In controlled experiments, Sydney University psychologist Lyndon Rose found that the Australian bushmen consistently averaged better than fifty per cent correct in dice guessing tests. In one particularly impressive test, the psychologists placed a cigarette into a tightly sealed box. Three bushmen were asked to guess what the box contained. One slightly more sophisticated than the others, promptly told the researchers that the box contained a cigarette. The other two guessed that the box contained "tobacco and paper."

To increase the difficulty of the experiment, a cigarette holder was placed in the box and ten natives were chosen at random to guess the contents. Admitted separately to a sealed hut, the aborigines quickly responded to the challenge placed before them by the psychologists. Although none of them had never seen a cigarette holder before, nine of them precisely described the shape, length, and color of the unknown object.

Such field work is fascinating and is certainly in keeping with the best scientific tradition, especially in such areas as geology, botany, and biology. However, because so many reluctant members of the scientific establishment look askance at such findings, it behooves the parapsychologist to set up a number of tedious statistical tests in an effort to provide the skeptics with controlled and repeatable experiments. The most common of these tests consists of a series of card-guessing experiments.

The standard Zener, or ESP, cards consist of a deck of 25 cards, five each of five different symbols: a cross, a square, a circle, a star, and a pair of wavy lines. In *The Mind Readers: Some Recent Experiments in Telepathy,* Dr. S. G. Soal tells how a "psi" researcher evaluates such statistics. Although Dr. Soal grew weary of the standard designs and made a deck of his own consisting of five sets of brightly colored animals, the mathematical procedure is, of course, exactly the same.

"If the cards are well mixed," Dr. Soal tells us, "we should expect that an ordinary person who guesses through the pack would, on the average, make 5 correct guesses."

The parapsychologist is quick to point out that this assumes "that the guesser is not told whether his individual guess is right until he has finished his 25 guesses." It is apparent that if this precaution were not followed, an alert subject could quite easily keep count of the number of times that a particular symbol had turned up and adjust his subsequent guesses accordingly.

"When we say that the average score is 5/25," Dr. Soal continues, "this does not mean that a person with no telepathic ability will guess exactly 5 cards correctly every time. Generally he will get more or fewer than 5 cards right. But if he does the experiment say 30 times, adds up all his scores and divides the total by 30 the figure he arrives at will usually be very close to 5, say 5.3 or 4.7, and the more packs he runs through the closer his average score will approximate 5.

"It follows, therefore, that in a total of N guesses one would expect *on the average* to make N/5 'hits' or 'successes.' Thus if one guessed through 8 packs of cards, i.e., 200 trials, one would expect on an average to guess one-fifth, i.e., 40 of them correctly."

Statisticians term this average number, N/5, the "mean chance expectation." If instead of an average score of 40/200, a man scored 60 or 70, the difference between his actual score and the "expected" or "average" score is called the "deviation." The larger the deviation from the average score, the less likely it is that the high score is a mere chance fluctuation.

But the parapsychologist cannot rest his case by saying that this impressive deviation from chance has occurred. He must play the statisticians' game to the limit and compare this actual score with a figure known as the "standard deviation." Actual deviation over standard deviation gives the statistician the "critical ratio." The larger the critical ratio, or CR, the more likely that the deviation is due not to "chance" but to some cause, known or unknown.

Soal gives an example in which a subject hypothetically scores 64, or a CR of 4.2. The researcher's final step is to look up the CR on a normal probability table in order to determine what the "odds" are that this score is due to something other than chance.

According to Dr. Soal, "Consulting this . . . we find that for CR—4.0 the odds against chance are 15,770 to 1; for CR—4.5 the odds are 147,190 to 1. So that for CR—4.2 we can obtain a very rough interpolation, odds of about 50,000 to 1 against getting a *numerical* value of the CR as high as 4.2.

"This, of course, for all human purposes is fairly conclusive that some 'cause' other than 'chance' has been at work in our experiment."

The results of such exacting and exhausting laboratory experimentation have not been as conclusive as parapsychologists have hoped, nor, as we have previously mentioned, are the demonstrations of laboratory "psi" as dramatic as spontaneous ESP. Accumulated evidence has indicated, however, that telepathy is a talent, which nearly everyone has to a certain degree, and that it is a talent, like that of painting or singing, which can be developed with training and practice.

Although we shall deal with the testing and development of one's extrasensory abilities in a later chapter, we should mention here that any two people can arrange a series of elementary tests which can be conducted between them in an effort to determine their telepathic talents. Zener "ESP" cards are not difficult to obtain for card-guessing experiments. Another simple test is that of "transmitting" sketches. Designate yourselves as "agent" and "percipient" and seat yourselves at tables in separate rooms. The agent draws a picture at a previously agreed upon time, numbers it, then concentrates upon his sketch. The percipient, who is sitting with his blank sheet of paper, tries to put himself in as relaxed a mood as possible and in as receptive a state of mind as possible. When he feels that he has received an impression from the agent, the percipient sketches his interpretation of whatever has come to his mind. After a previously agreed upon time and number of transmissions have been achieved, the agent and percipient rejoin one another and compare the results.

An interesting aspect of this test may be noticed. It may happen that as the agent is concentrating upon his sketch, his mind may wander to a subject which has a greater emotional attraction for him. Therefore, the agent may have drawn a sketch of a bird, but the percipient may have sketched that diamond ring which the agent is wondering whether or not to purchase for his sweetheart.

In 1930, the novelist Upton Sinclair published a record of experiments in telepathically transmitted drawings, which had been conducted with his wife and his brother-in-law, R. I. Irwin.

Mrs. Sinclair was always the percipient, and when Irwin was the agent, he "transmitted" from over forty miles away. The agent would make a set of drawings of such simple items as a nest with eggs, a flower, a tree, and enclose each sketch in an opaque envelope. At the agreed upon time, or later, Mrs. Sinclair would lie down on a couch and allow her mind and body to enter a state of complete relaxation. Experience soon taught her that other levels of mind would attempt to "guess" the sketch and thereby often confuse the true information which would come from a deeper level of authentic knowledge.

Mrs. Sinclair commented that for best results in such tests, one must develop the ability to hold in consciousness, without any sense of strain, a single idea, such as the petal of a flower. Association trains must not be allowed to develop, and, above all, no *thinking* about the idea must take place. A completely relaxed state of body and mind must be achieved.

It is difficult to measure the success of such tests with drawings, because often an idea associated with the drawing would come across rather than the actual sketch. In the Sinclair experiments of 290 drawings, 65 were judged successes, 155 partial successes, and 70 were failures.

Professor William McDougall said of the Sinclairs' experiments with their "mental radio," "The degree of success and the conditions of experiment were such that we can reject them as conclusive evidence of some mode of communication not at present explicable in accepted scientific terms, only by assuming that Mr. and Mrs. Sinclair either are grossly stupid, incompetent, and careless persons, or have deliberately entered upon a conspiracy to deceive the public."

My wife and I had an interesting experience with the spontaneous operation of our own "mental radios."

One morning I lay abed lightly dozing while my wife arose for a few minutes of peaceful contemplation before the children awakened. Being an avid follower of basketball, she picked up the sports pages and began to scan the results of a recent game. At the same moment, I had a visual image of sports copy as if the lines were coming across on some sort of teletype. Next, my "inner eye" swept a picture of action on the basketball court, then read the cutline beneath the photo. This was doubly strange to me, because while I sometimes glance at the results of an occasional football game, I follow only the progress of our local college basketball team.

When I got out of bed, I entered the living room and saw my wife curled up on the davenport reading the newspapers. I turned my back at once and asked her to turn to the sports section. When she assured me that she had, I then told her that I would "read" the story in the upper lefthand column. I recited as much of the sports copy as I could recall, then skipped to the picture and described the action in great detail. The cutline was especially vivid in my mind, and I proceeded to repeat it and as many of the other headlines scattered about the page as I could remember.

When I asked my wife to substantiate my recitation, she told me that my "reading" had been substantially correct. I had not, of course, repeated the story word for word, but my description of the photo was exact, even to the jersey numbers of the basketball players. My reading of the cutline had been almost letter perfect.

While we have not been able to effect such a dramatic transmission of information via the mental radio since that accidental broadcast, I should stress the point that the conditions on that particular morning were ideal. I lay in bed, not in a deep sleep, but in that completely relaxed moment before one truly awakens and begins a new day. This is the time when I find that the door to the deeper levels of my subconscious swings on well-oiled hinges—when I am in this almost somnambulistic state. Subsequent experimentations have been marred by too much conscious effort and physical distractions.

In 1924, Mrs. Henry Sidgwick, a prominent "psi" researcher, described a series of experiments conducted between 1910 and 1915 by Professor Gilbert Murray, of Oxford, and his daughter, Mrs. Arnold Toynbee, as "the most important ever brought to the notice of the Society for Psychical Research, both on account of their frequently brilliant success and on account of the eminence of the experimenter."

The procedure followed by Professor Murray is another that anyone interested in testing his own powers of telepathy can follow quite easily. Murray would leave the room and go out of earshot. Someone in the room—generally the Professor's eldest daughter, Mrs. Toynbee—would think of some scene or incident (or anything actually that came to her mind) and say it aloud so that the others in the room might hear it. The "thought" would be written down and Professor Murray would be summoned.

Upon returning to the room, Professor Murray would take hold of his daughter's hand and then proceed to describe in detail what had been described. "Psi" researchers have often noticed that a percipient's mind will respond much better to one agent than another and will also respond better in pleasant and warm surroundings. The Oxford professor was no exception to the general rule that a person gifted with ESP will perform more effectively when there is no hostility or skepticism present among the witnesses. Murray told the Society:

"The least disturbance of our customary method, change of time or place, presence of strangers, controversy and especially noise, is apt to make things go wrong. I become myself somewhat over-sensitive and irritable . . .

"When I am getting at the thing which I wish to discover, the only effort I make is a sort of effort of attention of a quite general kind. The thing may come through practically any sense channel, or it may discover a road of its own, a chain of reasoning or of association, which, as far as I remember, never coincides with any similar chain in the mind of anyone present, but is invented, for the purpose of the moment."

Let us witness a few examples from one series of experiments conducted by Professor Murray on a particular evening.

After he has left the room, Mrs. Toynbee rises to act as agent. She tells the group that she is thinking of her infant son, Tony, and of Helena Cornford's infant daughter and that both children are grown up and walking beside the river at Cambridge. Certainly this "thought" deals with concepts decidedly more difficult than a "bright red ball," or "a nest with eggs in it."

Professor Murray is brought back into the room. His

daughter tells him that she is the agent, and he takes her by the hand.

"This is not a book," he says after a moment. "It's got a sort of Cambridge feel in it. It's the Cornfords somehow. No, it's a girl walking beside the river, but it isn't Mrs. Cornford. Oh! It's baby Cornford grown up!"

"Who is she with?" his daughter prods.

"No," Murray shakes his head, "I don't get who she is with. No, I should only be guessing."

"Go on!" insist the assembled friends in the room.

"No," Murray smiles. "I should only think of another baby grown up—Tony."

In another experiment, Mrs. Toynbee announced that she was thinking of a real friend, Rupert Brooke, meeting the fictional character Natascha, heroine of Tolstoy's novel, *War and Peace,* and that Natascha was running through a wood and wearing a yellow dress.

As soon as Professor Murray grasped his daughter's hand, he said: "Well, I thought when I came into the room it was about Rupert. Yes, it's fantastic. He's meeting somebody out of a book. He's meeting Natascha in *War and Peace.* I don't know what he is saying—perhaps 'Will you run away with me?' "

"Can't you get the scene?"

"I should say it was in a wood."

"What color is Natascha's dress?"

"No, I can't get it."

Critics of Professor Murray's tests protested that hyper-acute hearing could account for his astonishing success at "reading" the thoughts of the various agents. Although Murray was escorted to a room far enough removed from the test room to convince all but the most dogged skeptics that he could not possibly have overheard any of the announced thoughts, "psi" researchers admitted the possibility of Murray passing into a state of hyperaesthesia that may have allowed him to catch the rhythm of a sentence, but not the complete idea. Granted that in some cases Murray (whose ordinary hearing was judged to be normal) might have developed some super-sonic hearing, hyperaesthesia can hardly be accepted as a general explanation of Murray's high rate of success in the experiments. There were, for example, many instances in which the professor received correct impressions of things that had not been mentioned by the agent in stating the "thought" to be transmitted.

Once Mrs. Toynbee named the scene in the novel *Greenmantle* in which a German peasant woman takes the principals in out of a snowstorm.

Professor Murray entered the room, touched Mrs. Toynbee's hand, and said that the scene was from literature, but from some book that he himself had not read. "It's a snowstorm," he went on. "It's somebody—I think it is a peasant woman giving shelter to a spy . . . I think it's a German peasant woman. The spy is an Englishman. I think it is a book of adventure."

The fact that the hero of *Greenmantle* is both an Englishman and a spy had not been mentioned when Mrs. Toynbee announced the thought that would be transmitted.

In other cases, Professor Murray seemed to get at the idea via a sensory impression. During one session, Patrick Murray announced that in his role as agent he would think of "the lion in the zoo trying to reach a large piece of meat just outside the cage."

When the professor was summoned and took hold of Patrick's hand, he declared: "A sort of smell of wild animals—carnivorous animals. Something grabbing through bars at a piece of meat at a zoo. Don't know the animal."

Again, even though Professor Murray did not get an image of the particular animal involved in the thought, he received a distinct impression of the action of the thought and even a sense of the smell characteristic of the zoo.

Rene Warcollier, a chemical engineer who has been president of the *Institut Metapsychique* since 1950, experimented with telepathic sketch transmissions for over ten years. Enlisting the aid of a number of friends, Warcollier scattered various duos about Paris, designating one as agent, the other as percipient. Although a line by line duplication of the agent's drawings occurred in only a small percentage of the experiments, Warcollier and his friends concluded that more than half of the trials produced meaningful responses.

In addition to re-emphasizing the establishment of telepathy as a genuine phenomenon, they noticed a number of interesting aspects of this particular "psi" function. They discovered, for example, that motion played a major part in the telepathic transmission of the drawings. Often what came through was not an exact photographic duplicate of the agent's original, but an image that had been rearranged into a new pattern. A square, for instance, may have come across as four scattered right angles.

Warcollier's experimenters also determined that pictures with strong emotional content were more readily perceived than those of abstract or intellectual concept. No image seemed to be instantly received by the percipients. In some cases, several minutes would pass before the idea would intrude into consciousness.

Experiments have been conducted with individuals who have been placed in hypnotic trance and told that they have telepathic rapport with each other.

On the evening of April 17, 1958, Hyman Arthur Lewis, Director of the Michigan Hypnosis Institute and a Fellow of the American Society for Psychical Research, headed a. test involving Geraldine Ann Glaser, 20, and Robert Topolevski, 35. Topolevski is also an accomplished hypnotist.

Separated by approximately sixty feet, the subjects were placed in hypnotic trance. Robert was told that he was able to open his eyes but was instructed to remain in trance. He was handed paper and a pen and told to visualize any picture that came to his mind and to draw it on the paper. After he had sketched an object, he was asked to stare at the picture. The hypnotist, Don Meyers, then told him that he was capable of transmitting this visual image to Geraldine Ann.

After Robert had begun to concentrate on the sketch, Meyers signaled Lewis, who was with Miss Glaser, to prepare the woman to receive Robert's telepathic impulse. Lewis told the hypnotized Miss Glaser that she was in direct rapport with Robert and that she would receive an impression from him that she should draw on the paper before her.

During the course of the experiment, which lasted about an hour and a half, several drawings of astonishing similarity were produced by the couple who had been placed in hypnotic rapport.

Laboratory tests have indicated a number of interesting facts concerning the conditions under which telepathy —and, in general, all testable "psi" phenomena—work.

Distance seems to have no effect on telepathy or clairvoyance. Equally remarkable results have been achieved when the percipient was a yard away from the agent or when the experimenters were separated by several hundred miles. Dr. S. G. Soal, the British researcher who has conducted extensive tests with "mind-readers," has written:

"In telepathic communication it is personality, or the linkage of personalities, which counts, and not spatial separation of bodies. This is what we might expect on the assumption that brains have spatial location and spatial extension, but that minds are not spatial entities at all.

"If this is true then there is no sense in talking about the distance between two minds, and we must consider brains as focal points in space at which Mind produces physical manifestations in its inter-action with matter."

"Psi" researchers have learned that the percipient's attitude is of great importance in achieving high ESP scores. Personalities do enter into "psi" testing even as they do into other aspects of human relationships. A cheerful, informal atmosphere that is as un-laboratory-like as possible, encourages the successful functioning of ESP. It has also been demonstrated that those who "believe" in their "psi" powers score consistently higher than those skeptics who regard it all as a lot of nonsense.

Although the agent in the laboratory must be careful to create and foster a friendly and cheerful atmosphere, spontaneous "psi" seems to work best under conditions which Dr. Jan Ehrenwald terms a "state of psychological inadequacy." Naming this state of "psi" readiness the "minus function," Dr. Ehrenwald believes that "a necessary condition for telepathic functioning is a state of inadequacy or deficiency such as loss or clouding of consciousness (sleep, hypnosis, trance, fever, brain defects)."

The "psi" researcher faces another risk in the laboratory when he is engaged in the long-term testing of a percipient: the decline effects in ESP that can be brought on by sheer boredom in the method of testing. The exercise of "psi" ability does sap psychic energy and even excellent performers invariably score higher when they are fresh. Once the novelty of the test has worn off, the interests of the percipient wander elsewhere, and so, apparently, does his ESP. Once again one is reminded of the difficulty of forcing "psi" into the laboratory in strenuous attempts to satisfy orthodox science's demand for controlled and repeatable experiments.

It is interesting to note that, on the average, a man is more effective as an agent and a woman is more effective as the percipient. This seems to apply to spontaneous instances of telepathy and other functions of "psi" as well as to roles assumed under laboratory conditions. Laboratory tests also demonstrate that percipients often achieve better results if the agent is of the opposite sex. Perhaps this is one more indication that "psi" is a fundamental and natural force that must be included in any total concept of man and his world.

5.

CLAIRVOYANCE, COPS, AND
DOWSING RODS

The body of 17-year-old Van Allen, Jr., of Jackson, Mississippi, had been lost for eight days when, on the night of April 11, 1964, Mrs. James F. "Billy" Runnels had her dream.

Mrs. Runnels and her husband had joined the searchers on that day, and had returned, weary and in despair that the body of the youth would never be recovered. He had drowned in the Pearl, a treacherous river known to be full of sink holes and whirlpools that had sucked many humans and animals down to a watery death. More than one victim's body had never been recovered. Regrettably, it appeared as though that would be the case with the body of the unfortunate teen-ager.

Then, as she lay drifting off into sleep, Mrs. Runnels suddenly "saw" and immediately recognized a particular curve of river three miles south of the city water works dam. There, caught on a log in midstream, Mrs. Runnels saw Van's body, clad in blue swim trunks.

Mrs. Runnels sat up in bed and told her dream to her husband. She waved down his protests that searchers had already passed that spot a dozen times without seeing a thing. The dream had seemed so real, that Mrs. Runnels insisted they put out their boat in the morning and investigate.

The next morning, accompanied by a young neighbor, Wyatt Bridges, the Runnels launched their boat in the midst of a driving rainstorm. Then, as they rounded the river bend which she had seen in her dream, Mrs. Runnels caught a flash of blue near a log. As they neared the log in midstream, they saw the body of Van Allen, Jr., just as it had appeared in Mrs. Runnels' dream.

"I have never experienced this sort of thing before," Mrs. Runnels later told newsmen. "The whole thing, the dream and then finding the boy's body, gave me an eerie and queer feeling."

Eerie though such an experience may be to the percipient, a clairvoyant dream is by no means uncommon. Factually substantiated reports abound confirming clairvoyant dreams that have led to the discovery of a missing child, the location of a lost object of value, or the recovery of a corpse. There seems little room for doubt that dreams may sometimes be clairvoyant and precognitive.

In early March of 1964, Dennis Hargus, a nine-year-old boy from Mesa, Arizona, was lost in the mountains near Prescott, Arizona. He had wandered away from breakfast at the YMCA camp near Groom Creek, and when it occurred to the boy that he might be lost, he remembered how his parents had always stressed that if he should one day find himself in such a predicament he should stop and think, and not panic.

Dennis made his way to the top of Maverick Mountain, "So I could look down and see where I was." He fashioned a crude brush shelter next to a large log, crawled in, and pulled his sweatshirt over his head, because: "I was afraid of the dark."

If Dennis had been older, he might perhaps have become frightened to the point of panic, by the dropping temperature. That night it chilled to 12°. Dennis' parents, the counselors at the YMCA camp, and volunteer searchers reluctantly called a halt to the search until morning. Rugged terrain made searching after dark an impossibility.

Virgil Maxwell, a retired rancher, shut off the news on the radio and shook his head sadly. He was aware of what a night's exposure could do to the lost boy, and he was worried. If only there was something that he could do to help little Dennis.

Still thinking of the lost boy, Virgil Maxwell prepared for bed and, after several restless minutes, fell asleep. During the night, the retired rancher had a vivid dream of the lost boy. He saw that he was on Maverick Mountain and recognized the general area. In his dream, the boy was caught on a white picket fence and could not get loose.

Early the next morning, Maxwell saddled his horse and headed directly for the spot which he had seen in his dream. He called out the boy's name, and Dennis answered: "Who is it?"

The rancher carried Dennis down the mountain to his waiting family. The boy's trouser legs were frozen stiff and colored with frost—symbolized, perhaps, by the "white picket fence" in Maxwell's dream.

"I dreamed right where he was," Maxwell told the boy's grateful parents.

The way in which sleep or a trance-like state opens the door to the subconscious of man, wherein lies the power and knowledge of the transcendent self, has been observed many times.

In 1849, the famous mathematician, Augustus de Morgan, wrote of his first experience with what came to be known as "traveling clairvoyance." The early mesmerists (hypnotists) carried out a great many experiments during which the subject would be asked to "go somewhere" mentally and to describe what he saw. Some truly astonishing reports come out of these early experiments. It is regrettable that such tests were not encouraged by the scientific establishment.

In the particular experiment of which De Morgan wrote, the mathematician told of dining at a friend's house which was about a mile from his own. De Morgan's wife was not present, having remained at home to treat a young epileptic girl with mesmeric therapy. When De Morgan returned to his home, his wife greeted him with the words: "We have been after you." While in a hypnotic trance the girl—whose clairvoyant abilities had been demonstrated on numerous other occasions—had been instructed to "follow Mr. De Morgan."

When the girl's mother had heard the name of the street on which the mathematician could be located, she told Mrs. De Morgan, "She'll never find her way there. She's never been so far away from Camden Town."

In a moment, the girl announced that she stood before the house. Mrs. De Morgan told her that she should knock at the door and go in. The hypnotized clairvoyant answered by saying that she could not knock at the door until she had entered the gate. Mrs. De Morgan was puzzled at this, and it was only upon Mr. De Morgan's return that the mystery was explained. Having never been to this particular friend's house, Mrs. De Morgan was not aware of the fact that the house stood in a garden and that the front door was reached only after one had entered at the garden gate. But the hypnotist bade her subject to simulate entering the house and continue in her pursuit of Mr. De Morgan.

The girl said that she was inside the house and could hear voices upstairs. She "walked" up the stairs and gave a detailed description of the people assembled, the furniture, objects, pictures in the room, and the colors of the drapes and curtains. De Morgan, admittedly awed by the clairvoyantly gained information, verified that each detail was precise and exact. He was even more astonished when the girl repeated the conversations she had overheard and described the dinner menu.

The Netherlands' Gerard Croiset is one of the most gifted clairvoyants in the world today. Perhaps the most remarkable of the many experiments that have been conducted with Croiset is a seemingly endless series of chair tests.

Devised for Croiset nineteen years ago by Professor Tenhaeff of the Dutch Society for Psychical Research, the test was first accomplished by the clairvoyant in October of 1947. From the very outset the results were startling; Croiset has since repeated the experiment several hundred times before scientists in five European nations.

The test itself is conducted quite simply. Croiset is taken to a theater, an auditorium, or a meeting house, where a chair number is selected completely at random by a disinterested third party. Croiset then predicts, anywhere from one hour to twenty-six days, who will sit in the chair. The descriptions given by the paragnost (as such sensitives are called in Holland) are never vague and generalized but quite exact and astonishingly detailed. Often, not only is the individual's appearance described but also characteristics of his personality and even certain emotional difficulties which the subject may be experiencing at the time. Sometimes Croiset sees the subject's past and is able to predict things about the person's future.

Another brilliant Dutch clairvoyant, Peter Hurkos, manifested latent powers after he had suffered a fractured skull in June, 1943. After the Second World War, Hurkos began to devote most of his time to psychic crime detection.

In one of his first cases as a psychic sleuth working with police, Hurkos had only to hold the coat of a dead man to be able to describe the man's murderer in detail that included the assailant's eye glasses, mustache, and wooden leg. When police admitted that they already had such a man in custody, Hurkos told them where the man had hidden the murder weapon.

In June 1964, Croiset was consulted in the murder case of the three Mississippi civil-rights workers, James Chaney, Andrew Goodman, and Michael Schwerner. Via trans-Atlantic telephone wire, Croiset accurately described the area where the three young men's bodies would be found and correctly implicated the local law enforcement officers as participants in the slayings. Although the FBI later made no formal acknowledgment of the clairvoyant's aid in the case, according to writer Jack Harrison Pollack, the law enforcement officers actively sought information from the Utrecht sensitive.

Clairvoyants have been co-operating with law enforcement agencies for years, but usually, as it is meticulously pointed out, in an "unofficial" capacity, the Dutch police being among the very few official agencies who openly consult clairvoyants for assistance in crime detection. In the United States, England, Canada, in spite of some astonishing results achieved with the help of psychics, the official policy is to discuss such important co-operation only in "off the record" interviews and unofficial statements. Even the most skeptical, however, must acknowledge that cases like the following rise above the level of sheer guesswork and make a strong case in favor of spontaneous "psi" phenomena.

When Charles King shot his partner, Edward Hayward, in the Alberta woods on a moonlit night in September, 1904, the greedy prospector made absolutely certain that there were no witnesses to his vicious betrayal. Being a practical materialist, Charles King could not possibly have guessed that a witness to the murder existed more than six thousand miles from the scene of the crime. Back in England, the victim's brother, George Hayward, had, in a dream, "seen" the murder committed as vividly as if he had been an on-the-spot witness.

When word of his brother's murder reached England, George Hayward reported his dream and it provided the necessary lead for officials to arrest Charles King. George Hayward went to Canada to attend the trial, but his testimony was not admitted into court records. Everyone connected with the investigation remarked, however, that the dream had been a remarkable coincidence.

In 1930, another remarkable "coincidence" occurred

when Professor Gladstone, a mentalist, paused in the course of his act in a theater in Beechy, Saskatchewan, pointed to a man in the audience and said: "Your friend Scotty McLaughlin has been murdered."

His pointing forefinger next found Constable Carey of the Royal Mounted Police seated amidst the wide-eyed audience and told him: "And you are the man who will find his body. I will be with you when you do."

The next morning, the mentalist directed the officer to the murdered man's farm, described the death scene in detail, and led investigators to the spot in a field where the victim's corpse had been buried.

A number of law enforcement officers have discovered themselves to possess clairvoyant powers. Patrolman Don Sabel of Grosse Pointe Woods, Michigan, is an officer with an uncanny knack for solving crimes before they have been officially reported.

One fall evening in 1960, Patrolman Sabel and his partner, Robert Sass, picked up the alert of a holdup. According to the squawk box in their patrol car, Mr. and Mrs. Leslie Lambardi had been accosted in their home and robbed of a considerable amount of cash and jewelry. In their shock and excitement, the couple was unable to give an accurate description of the bandit.

"Can't blame the folks," Patrolman Sass sighed, "but they haven't made our job any easier by not being able to describe the thief. It may take quite a while to grab this character."

"Turn the car around!" Sabel suddenly shouted, a note of urgency in his voice.

Patrolman Sass blinked, did as his partner had asked. It was a warm evening for Michigan in autumn, and the streets were filled with men and women strolling and window shopping. Sass was unable to notice anything unusual that may have accounted for his fellow officer's sudden excitement.

"Here," Patrolman Sabel nodded his head. "Stop here." Without another word, the officer was on the street. He approached a man who was about to enter a restaurant and ordered him to halt. On his person, the man carried $500 in cash and a woman's wrist watch. Startled, he confessed at once to having committed the Lambardi holdup.

About two months later, Patrolman Sabel had another one of his "hunches" when he brought two men in for questioning. The nervous men felt as though they had stepped into some kind of "twilight zone" as the cop with all the answers began to grill them. It was crazy! It was weird! But the patrolman knew everything they had done that night.

Just as Patrolman Sabel was completing his interrogation, Mr. and Mrs. John Herberling phoned the station house to report that they had returned from an evening out and discovered that their home had been burglarized. The police chief was able to inform the astonished Herberlings that Patrolman Sabel had already arrested the culprits and had just obtained their confessions.

Clairvoyant dreams and "hunches," although never accepted officially into police records, are usually given some respectful attention and, if they prove to be accurate, are at least granted the pseudo-dignity of being termed "a coincidence." A "professional" clairvoyant, however, may run a certain risk when he offers his services to the police.

The celebrated Edgar Cayce, an incredibly gifted clairvoyant, who used his talents primarily in the diagnosis of diseases, was once consulted in a murder case. Cayce, while in trance, recreated the scene in minute detail and identified the murdered girl's sister as her slayer. When law enforcement officers followed up the lead, they were astonished to find themselves with a confessed murderer on their hands. Cayce's satisfaction in aiding the police was soon dimmed when an officer appeared with a warrant for his arrest. The police chief had reasoned that the only way that the psychic could have known so much about the murder was to have somehow been an accomplice. Only rapid-fire talk of "psi" and the testimony of several corroborating witnesses allowed the befuddled police chief to retreat to his customary bailiwick.

A similar incident occurred to a young Norwegian psychic named Ingeborg Dahl. The young woman had demonstrated remarkable ability with predictive and clairvoyant automatic writing and had been encouraged by some close friends to develop her "psi" talents. Others, however, felt that Ingeborg's predictions were pure luck and coincidence and that she had no genuine psychic abilities at all. These skeptics were shocked at the girl's "bad taste" when she declared that she foresaw her own father's death by drowning.

In the summer of 1934, the elderly retired judge was seized with cramps while swimming at Hanko, and Ingeborg Dahl's prediction came true. But the daughter had not foreseen the bizarre turn of events that followed her father's death. The same skeptics who had once laughed off her predictions as coincidences, then charged her with the murder of her father. According to their allegations, she had drowned her father in an attempt to prove her prophetic powers.

For a time, the trial of Ingeborg Dahl greatly resembled that of a medieval witch hunt. Representatives from the Norwegian Society for Psychical Research were denied the right to offer expert testimony in order not to offend the scientific establishment. Fortunately for Ingeborg Dahl, the prosecution was unable to develop enough solid evidence to support a murder charge. After an extended trial, it was decided that Judge Dahl's own presentiment of death may have produced a kind of hypnotic suggestion that led to his drowning.

Perhaps one clairvoyant had such hazards in mind when he recently told me: "People must be very cautious when they go about developing their powers of clairvoyancy. True that these powers lie latent within all and can be encouraged, but I really feel that one should not consciously cultivate such talents. If God wishes an individual to be clairvoyant, this ability will develop in spite of the individual. Possessing this gift can be a trial, however. Our society just isn't ready for it yet."

Powerful emotions like fear and dread, coupled with the pain of injury or death—all seem to be important aids to the clairvoyant in receiving extrasensory impressions of the missing, the murdered, and the victims of misdeeds. When these powerful elements are removed, the clairvoyant is often unable to make any positive "connection" with the case in question. It has been noted, for instance, that when a psychometrist has been given an object belonging to an insane person, the sensitive's impressions reflect the same jumbled thinking as the subject. Missing persons suffering from amnesia are also difficult to make "contact" with, because in such cases the "fear signals" are not being broadcast.

Remarkable use of psychics has been made by police agencies around the world. Whether or not this fact is made mention of in official reports is perhaps immaterial, as long as the talents of these gifted people are being utilized. One would hope, though, that some day soon, "psi" phenomena will have its official day in court and be acknowledged as the magnificent mental tool it has so often proved to be.

Another "unofficial" ESP ability that the common man has utilized for centuries is that of dowsing for water with the forked stick. Few manifestations of "psi" have been more hotly debated than that of dowsing. On the one hand is the pronunciamento of the scientific establishment, which declares that locating water by means of a forked stick is utter nonsense. On the other side of the argument are those men and women who go about locating water with their forked maple twigs, completely impervious to the ridicule visited upon them by the skeptics. They could not care less whether or not a laboratory technician believes that water cannot be located in such a manner. All they know is that it works and that they have been finding water in just that way for years.

Novelist Kenneth Roberts stated in his book, *Henry Gross and His Dowsing Rod,* "Not all the derision of all the geologists in the world can in any way alter the unfailing accuracy of the dowsing rod in Henry Gross's hands. Not all the cries of 'hokum,' 'curious superstition,' 'fanciful delusion,' 'hoax,' 'witchery,' 'pseudo-science,' can destroy or even lessen the value of Henry's dowsing . . ."

I have included dowsing in the general realm of clairvoyance, because, to me, the twig in the hand must serve as a stimulant to the greater knowledge of the transcendent self in much the same manner as the photograph of a missing child serves to establish psychic rapport for the clairvoyant power of the psychometrist.

The *modus operandi* of the dowser seldom varies. He grasps the ends of a twig firmly (I have been told that peach, apple, and maple seem to work best) with palms upward. As he starts his search for water, he carries the butt of the stick pointed upward. When he nears water, he can feel the pull as the butt end begins to dip downward. When the dowser is over the water, the twig has been bent straight down, having turned through an arc of 180 degrees. A stick of brittle wood will break under the grip of a dowser as the butt moves downward. Pliable twigs will twist themselves down despite an effort to hold them straight.

For nearly twenty years, the town officials of Swampscott, Massachusetts, sought a lost water supply, until, in the summer of 1963, after modern methods of detection had failed, they applied the ancient technique of dowsing with immediate success.

Swampscott's administrative buildings are housed in the former mansion of the late Elihu Thomson, co-founder of General Electric Company. Each summer, the residents of the town had been forced to ration their water supply. Old-timers said that Professor Thomson had located an independent supply of water, but no one could remember where it was. Ever since Swampscott had purchased the old mansion in 1944, the Department of Public Works had conducted a diligent search for the underground water supply. Nothing had worked—including a mine detector —and the townspeople were about ready to give up.

Then, half-jokingly, someone suggested dowsing. Superintendent of Public Works Paul A. Polisson was skeptical, but he decided that they had tried everything else. Fifteen minutes after Polisson and a group of men had set out with forked twigs in their hands, "Dutchy" Emery, a 56-year-old laborer, located the lost water supply.

Later, his companions testified that the stick had moved downward with such force that it had scraped skin off Emery's thumb.

A back hoe operator dug a hole nearly five feet deep at the spot where Emery's bending twig had indicated. In awe, the men stared at the pipe that had been unearthed. Polisson wrenched a cap off the pipe and dropped a weighted string into the opening. There was twenty-eight feet of pure spring water in the pipe, enough to get the lawns of Swampscott through the worst drought.

Nearly twenty years of digging and searching had accomplished nothing. In fifteen minutes, an amateur dowser with a determined twig and a scraped thumb had located a lost water supply. A scientific explanation? There is none. Not in acceptable scientific jargon. As in all "psi" phenomena, the answer lies in the subconscious power of the transcendent self. Henry Gross, the greatest practitioner of dowsing the world has ever known, located water on parched Bermuda by dowsing a map of the island spread on the floor of his home in Maine.

In 1953, UNESCO sponsored a committee of prominent European scientists in their study of radiesthesia (dowsing). Their carefully considered report was that "there can be no doubt that it is a fact."

The *Academie des Sciences* of Paris has commented:

"It is impossible to deny the existence of the power, although its nature cannot be determined."

Five Nobel Prize winners have endorsed dowsing, and so has the Institute of Technical Physics of the Dutch National Research Council.

Well-watered herds of cattle and prospering communities in the dry Southwest offer impressive testimony to the prowess of the dowser. Yet, because not *everyone* can do it in a controlled and repeatable experiment, dowsing is denied general scientific acceptance.

6.

POLTERGEISTS, PSYCHOKINESIS, AND
THE TELEGRAPH KEY IN
THE SOAP BUBBLE

The first manifestations in the office of court reporter George Wheeler concerned themselves with the telephones.

According to Mrs. Helen Rosenberg, the row of lights on the base of each telephone would blink in rapid succession, but there would be no one on the line. The Oakland, California, telephone company insisted that there was nothing wrong with the instruments in the office at 1904 Franklin Street.

The electric typewriters were the next victims of the weird pranks. The coil springs beneath the keys began to twist together and ball up. The typewriter repairmen left loan machines that suffered the same mysterious mechanical malady.

"Those springs normally last for the life of the machine," said Bob Goosey, a sales representative for the Royal McBee typewriter company. "We haven't replaced three of those springs in the last ten years. But during the past few days, we've replaced about a hundred in Wheeler's machines. We've practically exhausted our stock of springs in the Bay area."

By June 15, 1964, when vases began to fly across the room, telephones began leaping from desks, and ashtrays began shattering, George Wheeler and his staff reluctantly concluded that a poltergeist had come to their office.

Jim Hazelwood, editorial writer for the Oakland *Trib-*

une, kept a journal of sixty fantastic minutes in the psychically super-charged office.

10:30 A.M. Metal dictaphone foot pedal with cord wrapped around it flew out of the cabinet, struck a wooden counter and fell to the floor . . .

10:35 A.M. Light bulbs broke in stairwell between third and fourth floors. Base of bulb was on the stair with the glass, indicating that the bulb had been unscrewed. No footsteps heard or anyone seen in hallways.

10:40 A.M. Heard noise in Mr. Wheeler's office which was vacant. Discovered can of liquid wax on floor, about eight feet from cupboard where it is kept.

10:45 A.M. Loud noise in vacant office where water cooler is kept. Rushed in immediately to find metal cup container lying on floor approximately ten feet from cooler. Paper cups were strewn around the floor. No chance for anyone to leave the room without being seen by me.

10:50 A.M. Door which had been removed from hinges on the previous day to permit moving desks, suddenly toppled over with a loud crash . . .

11:05 A.M. . . . metal card index file . . . landed on the floor with a loud bang. It had been sitting on a metal filing case where I had placed it earlier. There was no one in the room. The first thing that I had done on entering the office that morning had been to place the metal index box on top of the filing case to see if it would fall. It did.

11:10 A.M. Metal and plastic top of typewriter flew out of the open window . . . and clattered to the street below where Dr. F. J. Stryble was walking. Dr. Stryble returned the typewriter top to us.

11:13 A.M. Arrival of two physicists with equipment for testing radiation. They found none.

11:30 A.M. A two-pound can of coffee flew out of the cupboard and landed about ten feet from the shelves in Mr. Wheeler's office. The plastic top of the can came loose and a handful of coffee was spilled. I was the first one in the room. There was no one there.

Mr. Irv Dickey, a former president of the California Society for Psychical Study, termed the "haunted office" a classic poltergeist case "except for one thing. When the poltergeist phenomenon occurs, it is usually in the presence of an adolescent child. If the child is removed from the location, the phenomenon stops. In this case, there doesn't seem to be a child involved."

Dr. Arthur Hastings, an active "psi" researcher, commented to the press that this was the first time that he had ever heard of a poltergeist case taking place in an office.

On June 17th, the phenomena seemed to reach a climax shortly after two staff members had entered the office that morning. In a flurry of mad activity, the water cooler tipped over, a large wooden cabinet came crashing down, and a movable counter flipped over onto its back.

"This is usually the pattern with poltergeist phenomena," Dr. Hastings told newsman Hazelwood. "They start slowly, build up to a climax, and then stop altogether. I don't think we'll see any more of these occurrences."

Dr. Hastings' evaluation was accurate for nine days, then, on June 26th, the poltergeist was once again busy with its annoying psychic pranks.

"When springs started breaking in all three typewriters," Mrs. Rosenberg sighed, "I knew that it had come back."

Mrs. Rosenberg quickly moved about the office, trying to place all breakable objects on the floor before the invisible jokester had an opportunity to send them shattering. Her preventive maneuvers did little good. A cup that she had just set down leaped eight feet across the room and shattered against a filing cabinet. Two glass ashtrays crashed to the floor, and a stapler bounced across a desktop.

Dr. Hastings assured the beleaguered office staff that the "eye of the storm had passed on and only the weaker manifestations remain." It appeared that the investigator's appraisal was correct. After that last dramatic activity, the poltergeist's energy seemed to have dissipated.

Poltergeist (German for "noisy ghost") manifestations are dramatic instances of psychokinesis on the rampage. The psychokinetic activity of the poltergeist is as measurable and as demonstrable and as trackable as a sputnik in the sky, the Northern Lights, or the photosynthesis of plants. Although the pranks of the poltergeist were formerly attributed to malicious tricks perpetrated by demons and nasty disembodied spirits, the great majority of "psi" researchers today hold that some faculty of PK is at work.

"The poltergeist is not a ghost," Dr. Nandor Fodor, the late psychoanalyst, once wrote, "but a bundle of projected repressions."

Quite probably, the sex changes which occur during puberty have a great deal to do with the peculiar type of PK that is responsible for poltergeist activity. We have only begun to realize some of the vast chemical changes which take place in the body during adolescence. Who can say what may happen in the lower levels of the subconscious? "Psi" researchers have noted that more often a girl than a boy is at the center of poltergeistic disturbances and that the sexual change of puberty is associated with either the beginning or the termination of the phenomena. To refer back to the poltergeist-plagued office in Oakland, California, it should be mentioned that one of the staff was an extremely sensitive 20-year-old, who was adjusting to married life. Researchers have also observed that the sexual adjustments of the marital state can also trigger such phenomena.

The poltergeist often finds its energy center in the frustrated creativity of a brooding adolescent, who is denied accepted avenues of expression. This brings up the question of just where man's limits of creativity might lie? It seems a bit startling to most people to suggest that man's mind may be capable of bursting free of its three-dimensional bonds and utilizing specialized talents that virtually know no limits. It may be within the power of man's psyche to materialize other voices, other personalities, and junior psyches. It may be within the power of man's transcendent self to skip blithely over, around, or through the accepted barriers of space and time and to bring back tangible evidence of this strange journey in the form of objects which could only have been obtained in their place of native origin. The poltergeist seems to offer measurable, weighable, demonstrable proof of this psychic capacity. The tragedy in the poltergeist phenomena is that it illustrates a perverted or uncontrolled aspect of this incredible power.

One cannot deny that this energy force is directed by a measure of intelligence or purpose. Observers (skeptical scientists, hard-nosed newsmen, innocent bystanders alike) have reported seeing poltergeist-borne objects turn corners, poltergeist-manipulated chalk write intelligible sentences on walls, and poltergeist-flung pebbles come out of nowhere to strike children. But, as one investigator commented, "the phenomena are exactly such as would occur to the mind of a child or an ignorant person."

Sacheverell Sitwell wrote his observation that the poltergeist always directed its power toward "the secret or concealed weaknesses of the spirit . . . the obscene or erotic recesses of the soul. The mysteries of puberty, that trance or dozing of the psyche before it awakes into adult life, is a favorite playground for the poltergeist."

The perverse talents of the poltergeist range from the ability to toss pebbles and smash vases, to the astonishing ability to materialize human or beastlike entities, complete with voices, intelligent responses, and disagreeable odors. From man's earliest records to today's newspaper story, every reported poltergeist case follows precisely the same basic patterns. Cultural influences seem to matter little, if at all. A poltergeist manifestation is similar in character whether it takes place in Indonesia, Iceland, or Long Island. Only the interpretation of the disturbance varies. What is caused by the destructive impulse of a demon to one people, may be caused by the destructive impulse of a fragmented psyche to another.

Why it should be the baser elements of man's subconscious that find their expression in the poltergeist is a matter of great speculation among "psi" researchers. Physical violence is almost always expressed toward the adolescent energy center of the poltergeist, and a parent, a brother, or a sister may come in for his share of the punishment as well. If the poltergeist sticks around long enough (its average life is about two weeks) to develop a voice or the ability to communicate by raps or automatic writing, its communications are usually nonsensical, ribald, or downright obscene. In one famous American case, that of the Bell Witch of Springfield, Tennessee, the poltergeist was even responsible for the death of the father of Betsy Bell, a young woman who had suffered the onslaught of an invisible "witch" for four years from 1816 to 1820.

The Bell Witch developed into a powerful invisible entity that was capable of dealing violently with those who had come to expose the manifestations as some sort of trickery. "The blows were heard distinctly," one of the Bell family wrote in a diary, "like the open palm of a heavy hand."

From the moment the "witch" was possessed of a voice, it began to warn that John Bell's days were numbered. It had tormented both John and his daughter from the outset of the phenomena, but while it only punished Betsy for "transgressions," it malevolently pursued John at all times.

Dr. Nandor Fodor, in an attempt to "psychoanalyze" the Bell Witch, speculated that Betsy, approaching puberty, may have undergone a shocking sexual experience at the hands of her father. "It was probably to save her reason," Dr. Fodor theorized "that a fragment of her mind was split off and became the Bell Witch."

Conversely, the "witch" always treated Betsy's mother with respect and seemed genuinely solicitous of her health and well-being. Once when Mrs. Bell was ill, the entity materialized a quantity of hazelnuts and bade the woman to eat them. When Mrs. Bell complained that she had not the energy to crack them, the poltergeist swept them into the air and sorted the meats from the shells.

At a birthday party for Betsy, the "witch" treated the celebrants with a supply of fresh bananas. "I picked them myself in the West Indies," the voice crackled above their heads as it showered fruit down upon them.

As we have already noted, the poltergeist does strange things with time and space. We certainly do not need to stress the fact that bananas were a costly rarity in Tennessee in 1818. The notion that a farmer of only modest means would obtain such an expensive fruit for an extravagant prank seems untenable.

In December of 1820, John Bell was ill and confined to his bed. But even there, the "witch" would not allow him to rest. The poltergeist slapped his face, tossed his legs into the air, and jerked his bedclothes from his body.

On the morning of December 19th, John Bell lapsed into a stupor from which he never roused. John, Jr., noted a smoky-looking vial in the medicine cabinet in place of his father's regular prescription. A cat was given a small dosage and instantly dropped to the floor, convulsing horribly in its death throes.

"Where did this vial come from!" John, Jr., demanded.

"I put it there last night," the smug voice of the invisible "witch" told him. "I gave the old man a big dose of it while he was asleep. I fixed him!"

The disrespectful poltergeist sang bawdy songs during John Bell's funeral and made no secret of its joyous celebration.

As might be expected, the "witch's" strength began to decline sharply after the death of John Bell. The manifestations decreased steadily until spring, then ceased altogether, with a promise that "it" would return in seven years. True to its prophecy, the Bell Witch did reappear in 1828, but Betsy had married and moved away from the household. The remaining members of the family adopted a successful policy of ignoring the poltergeist, and the unwelcome guest at last faded into oblivion.

In some cases, the torment which the poltergeist visits upon its adolescent energy center is much more painful than the tugging of hair and the occasional slap of a cheek.

On May 10, 1951, an 18-year-old girl stumbled into police headquarters in Manila, Philippines, screaming that an "invisible monster" had been biting her.

Before the startled eyes of police officers, livid teeth marks appeared on the upper arms and shoulders of Clarita Villanueva. In an act of desperation, the officers—for a moment almost believing in the teen-ager's invisible monster—put Clarita into a jail cell. But the girl wailed that the monster was coming at her through the bars of the cell, and incredulous policemen stared openmouthed as red "teeth" marks appeared on her soft flesh.

The medical examiner was summoned and was forced to admit that the indentations certainly did look like the prints of teeth. The teen-ager was not drunk nor under the influence of any drug, the doctor observed after his examination.

On the following morning, the girl was brought to court to face charges of vagrancy which had been levied against her. There, before the astonished court, Clarita Villanueva suffered another attack from the "invisible beast." Reporters rushed to the girl's side, and the medical examiner took the girl in his arms.

"She is definitely not having an epileptic fit," he told

the newsmen, "and these teeth prints are real. But, as we can all testify, they are not self-inflicted."

Welts continued to appear on the girl's body. By the time that Mayor Lacson arrived, the wretched girl was a veritable mass of deeply embedded tooth prints, and her flesh was swollen and bruised. As the Mayor held one of Clarita's hands in his own, he was horrified to see deep marks appear on either side of her index finger.

The Mayor ordered the girl taken to the hospital, where, for some reason, the attacks ceased almost immediately. Perhaps some frustrated segment of Clarita Villanueva's subconscious felt the need to call attention to the conscious personality in some dramatic means, and, once this goal had been obtained, left the personality to fend for itself. It would seem, in the case of Clarita Villanueva, that the "teeth marks" were similar to the stigmata, which have been known to appear during heights of religious ecstasy.

One of the most unusual of all poltergeist manifestations occurred in 1931 on the Isle of Man. There, in the home of James T. Irving, the poltergeist not only developed a very articulate manner of speaking but claimed to be a mongoose that lived in a hole in the wall of their cottage. On a number of occasions, a rodentlike animal was seen by members of the family and by investigators, but the famous talking mongoose, which called itself Jef, preferred not to show itself to anyone.

A reporter for the Manchester *Daily Dispatch* asked his readers: "Have I ever heard a weasel speak? I do not know, but I do know that I heard, today, a voice I never imagined could issue from a human throat."

Jef maintained his home with the Irvings for nearly four years, spicing his stay by tossing objects at the family while they ate, squirting water at inquisitive reporters, and singing bawdy songs during his midnight forays.

Once Mrs. Irving reached her hand into Jef's hole and

stroked its fur. Not one for an open display of affection, the mongoose gave the woman a bite on the finger for her trouble. The fact that Mrs. Irving had actually touched the entity greatly excited Harry Price, the famous "psi" investigator. Price and his associates had just concluded that "Jef" was nothing but a disembodied voice. At his urging, the Irvings tried to persuade their strange boarder to stamp impressions of his feet in some plasticine blocks.

Jef obliged, but Mr. R. I. Peacock of the British Natural History Museum's Zoological Department was baffled by the impressions. "One print might have been made by a dog," he concluded. "The others are of no mammal known to me unless it is that of an American raccoon . . . certainly none of them was made by a mongoose."

In response to repeated requests to show itself openly rather than flitting about the cottage so mysteriously, Jef declared to Mrs. Irving: "If you saw me, you'd be petrified, mummified!"

A night with the assorted ghosts and poltergeists that made Borley Rectory their home petrified more than one inhabitant and "psi" researcher before the rectory burned to the ground in 1939. Called the most haunted house in England by investigator Harry Price, the complete range of poltergeist activity was observed within the walls of the rectory.

In 1937, after the last clergyman and his family had forsaken the eerie rectory, Price learned that the place was without an occupant. The investigator offered to rent the home as a kind of "ghost" laboratory. His terms were accepted, and Price set about enlisting a crew of forty investigators, who would take turns living in the rectory for a period of one year.

Those who volunteered to spend a year living with the Unknown were not disappointed. Immediately, mysterious pencil-like writings began to appear on the walls. Each time a new message was scribbled by the unseen fingers, it would be carefully encircled and dated. Two Oxford graduates testified that they observed new writing being formed even as they were busy ringing and dating another example.

Judging from the messages, it appeared that the entity had formed an attachment for Mrs. Marianne Morrison, the wife of the last clergyman who had lived in Borley Rectory. "Marianne . . . Marianne . . ." it scribbled over and over again. "Marianne . . . Light . . . Mass . . . prayers. Get light. Marianne . . . please . . . help . . . get."

The trained researchers were quick to locate a "cold spot" in one of the upstairs passages. Certain of the investigators testified that they experienced a feeling of faintness whenever they passed through it. Another cold spot was found on the landing outside of the Blue Room. The temperature of these areas was fixed at 48 degrees, regardless of what the temperature of the remainder of the rectory may have been.

One investigator saw the rectory's famous "nun" three times in one evening. A mysterious old cloak kept disappearing and reappearing in various rooms of the house. Nearly every one of Price's crew reported that he had been touched by invisible hands and had heard low, inaudible whisperings as they moved about the rectory.

Professor C. E. M. Joad of the University of London was one of the investigators who witnessed the eerie writings appearing on the walls. In the July, 1938, issue of *Harper's,* Joad wrote: ". . . having reflected long and carefully upon that squiggle, I did not and do not see how it could have been made by normal means . . . the universe must in some respects be totally other than what one is accustomed to suppose."

It is interesting to note that the poltergeist persisted in writing messages to "Marianne" even after Mrs. Morrison and her family had moved out of the rectory. When the Morrisons made their residence in Borley Rectory, the manifestations centered about Mrs. Morrison and the perplexed and frightened woman bore the brunt of the sometimes vicious haunting. One theory of poltergeistic activity maintains that a "psychic residue," a persistent, dynamic memory, can release itself when an individual of the right telepathic affinity comes upon the scene. In other words, the dormant poltergeistic influence can become reactivated when it discovers a sympathetic energy source in the psyche of a living person.

The incendiary activities of some poltergeists turn them into agents of constant terror. A poltergeist that hurls pebbles can be annoying; a disembodied voice may be eerie; but a poltergeist that rains down balls of fire is obviously dangerous.

One of the most dramatic incidents in which an incendiary poltergeist plays a prominent part occurred on the farm of John McDonald near Baldoon, Ontario. As many as fifty outbreaks of fire a day were extinguished by the anguished McDonalds and their anxious neighbors. A round-the-clock vigil was maintained and buckets of water were kept handy throughout the farmhouse and each of the outbuildings. Fires would start even on wet floors, and the wet planking would burn as if it had been coated with oil. The McDonalds and their neighbors ran until they were exhausted, dowsing smoldering planking and dodging new outbursts of flame. In spite of such vigilance, a fire broke out one morning while the McDonalds were eating breakfast and completely gutted their cabin. When the McDonalds moved, the invisible firebugs followed them, visiting similar fires on relatives and friends until the poltergeist eventually ran out of psychic fuel.

The awesome power of the human mind to, prism-like, focus energy and ignite fires may be yet another unknown ability of the subconscious self.

While visiting Memphis in 1927, Vice-President Dawes met a Negro laborer who could cause objects to burst into flame by breathing upon them.

Fourteen-year-old Jennie Bramwell of Toronto, Canada, and twelve-year-old Ann Kidner of Glasgow, Scotland, each had the power to ignite fires simply by concentrating on objects. Angry Glasgow farmers were on the verge of having Ann Kidner institutionalized, because haystacks erupted into flame at her very passing by on the road.

Cases of poltergeists pelting innocent families with stones and pebbles comprise by far the largest single category of poltergeistic phenomena and therefore seem to be the most common example of PK running wild. Ivan T. Sanderson, world-famous natural scientist, cautions us against using the term "throwing" when we speak of poltergeist activity. According to Sanderson's observations, the stones are "dropped" or "lobbed" or "just drift around" rather than thrown.

"Stone-dropping is a purely physical phenomenon," states Sanderson, "and can be explained on some physical principles, though not necessarily on Newtonian, Einsteinian, or any others that concern our particular space-time continuum."

Sanderson once marked some flying rocks in Sumatra and proceeded to play "catch" with them. The natural scientist insists that the rocks obey "some pattern that is not entirely random."

Although modern man may become just as startled by an onset of poltergeist phenomena as was his ancient or medieval counterpart, there is no reason to believe that a malignant or mischievous "spirit" is responsible for the activity. Data compiled by parapsychologists seem to demonstrate that the particular "entity" involved is a dissociated mental fragment (or Dr. Fodor's "projected bundle of repressions") that is motivated by primitive ideas and desires. Most often, the poltergeist occurs in a home in which there is an adolescent undergoing puberty or in which there are young people undergoing marital adjustment. There are a great many cases, however, where a psychic residue of bottled-up emotional energy may attach itself to some building or some particular locality. In these cases, only a sensitive person of the right telepathic affinity can trigger renewed poltergeist activity and physical phenomena.

Apart from the uncontrolled eruptions of psychokinetic power which we have examined in the poltergeist, there are individuals who have demonstrated the ability to discipline PK. Professional gamblers have long alleged that they can "make the dice obey" or make the little white ball in roulette stop wherever they wish.

Dr. J. B. Rhine began his experimental lab work in PK in 1934. Using dice-throwing experiments and utilizing several volunteers who claimed to have used "mind over matter" to bring in tangible rewards at the gaming tables, Dr. Rhine and his associates conducted tests and accumulated data until 1943 before they made any announcement of their results. In his *The Reach of the Mind,* Rhine sets forth an analysis of this data and concludes that psychokinesis has been established beyond all question. Although purists would exclude a chapter on PK from a book on ESP (clairvoyance, telepathy, are sensory types of phenomena, matter affecting mind; PK is a motor-type phenomenon, mind affecting matter), Rhine holds that the existence of one implies the existence of the other and that they are closely related phenomena.

In his series of tests, Rhine noted that dice-throwers with marked control over the dies were much more successful at the beginning of a run. The same sort of "decline" effect, that has been noted by agents testing telepathic percipients in card-guessing tests, was in evidence in testing for PK.

Other similarities existed between ESP and PK tests as observed in the Duke University parapsychology laboratories. For example, mechanical devices made no difference in the effectiveness of PK, and neither did distance. Once again, as in ESP testing, a relaxed, in-

formal atmosphere produced the best PK results. Another important similarity between the two paranormal
abilities is the fact that the person who expects success
and "believes" in his ability to produce the desired result
will always score much higher than the individual who
is indifferent to ESP or PK.

It appears that psychokinesis as well as extrasensory
perception is a talent that can be developed and encouraged and is an ability present, to a certain degree, in
all men.

A most remarkable test in PK was conducted by "psi"
researcher Harry Price in the National Laboratory for
Psychic Research in London. Price secured the co-
operation of a young woman who demonstrated an unusual facility for psychokinetic effects. She was not a professional medium and she did not request any money for
her time or services. The experiment had as its sole object
an attempt to offer scientific evidence that such a power
as PK did truly exist.

Price mounted a regular telegraph key inside a flat
metal bowl and set it on a stand. The telegraph key was
connected by means of heavily insulated wires to a
small, red electric light bulb, which was completely encased in a glass cover. When one pressed the telegraph
key, the circuit was completed and the red bulb lit up.
When the pressure on the key was removed, the lamp
went out.

Next Price prepared a mixture of glycerine and castile
soap and blew a bubble, which because of the addition of
the glycerine would last for hours, but because of its
fragile nature would burst at the slightest prodding. This
large soap bubble was placed over the telegraph key.
Over both the bubble and the key was set a transparent
glass cover. Not yet satisfied, Price next arranged a wire-
net cage around the glass cover, and, finally, placed a
larger, latticework cage of wood over the whole arrangement. Price now had one electric light bulb, encased in
glass and mounted on a stand, which, in turn, was con-

nected via wires to a telegraph key that was encased in a soap bubble, a glass cover, a wire cage, a larger wooden cage, and mounted on another stand.

The lights were dimmed at the request of the young lady, who stated simply that she preferred to work in semi-darkness.

During the course of the experiment, the telegraph key was pressed and the red light bulb flashed on and off several times.

When Price concluded the test, he found both cages as he had left them, the glass cover completely intact, and the soap bubble unbroken.

7.

PEOPLE WHO SEE WITHOUT EYES

Charlotte Young, a teacher in Spring Valley Junior High School, near San Diego, California, had her class take part in a parapsychological study. All of her pupils put on blindfolds and were asked to identify the colors of sheets of paper which she handed them. Alan Ames' identifications were almost 100 per cent correct.

The only way the young man could explain his astonishing score, was to say that he "saw" the colors that came under his hands. After the boy had proved his ability over and over again to unbelieving witnesses, word spread until a reporter from the *Saturday San Diego Union* came to investigate the lad. By the time the reporter began to follow the story, Alan could describe any article that was placed between his hands. To convince the reporter, Alan, while blindfolded, not only read the serial number on a dollar bill, he described the man's press card perfectly.

Alan Ames has the peculiar ability to perceive visual sensations without the use of his eyes. This ability, which is currently undergoing extensive research in both the United States and the Soviet Union, has been termed "Extra Ocular Vision" by those investigating the phenomenon. Even more amazing than simply being able to read with his hands, Alan Ames is also able to identify objects which are placed under opaque cloth. In some cases his hands can "see" where his eyes would fail.

In the Soviet Union the first wave of interest in EOV came after a young woman, Rosa Kuleshova, was able to distinguish colors with the use of the tips of her fingers.

She developed the ability on her own, practicing with the aid of her eyes. Although Kuleshova's case was the first to gain wide attention, many more individuals have been found who have such talent. Some are even more sensitive than Rosa.

The close association between this ability and clairvoyance cannot be denied. Yet EOV is rapidly coming under the scrutiny of traditional physics, biology, and psychology and, if the present trend continues, will soon be removed from the realm of parapsychology altogether. Some parapsychologists have scornfully suggested that these orthodox scientists have begun a study of psychic phenomena under the more respectable name of Extra Ocular Vision. Whatever the case, research with people who have light-sensitive portions of their skin is being carried on with increasing intensity in the U.S. and in the Soviet Union.

Several interesting explanations have been attempted, but none has been completely satisfactory. Once the ability had been discovered, experiments were performed to determine what forms of energy were being detected by the subject. Colors printed on all textures of cloth and paper were put under the sensitive fingers of Rosa Kuleshova, yet no matter what the texture, the girl was able to identify the color. Even when the color was placed under thin layers of glass, she was still very accurate. But when a thick plate of glass or plexiglas was placed between her fingers and the color, her accuracy fell sharply.

The Soviet experimenters next tested the girl's sensitivity to infra-red rays, which if intense enough, can be felt by any individual, because they raise the temperature of the skin. Soviet scientists made the intensity of the infra-red a thousand times greater than that of the normal colors which Rosa was to perceive. But, in this experiment, Rosa was unaware of the intense infra-red beam, and she again correctly picked out the colors which were arrayed before her.

In yet another Soviet experiment, a picture was projected on a screen and a blindfolded subject was asked to identify it. While normal light was used in the projector, the picture was identifiable. But the minute infra-red light was used, the subject lost contact with the form and the colors.

The conclusion, which the Russian scientists drew from these and other experiments, is that EOV is accomplished with the use of special sense receptors in the skin which are sensitive to electromagnetic radiation at the wave length of light. It seemed the only logical explanation.

Meanwhile in the U.S., Dr. Richard Youtz, a psychology teacher at Columbia University's Barnard College, has been leading the research. Working extensively with a Mrs. Stanley, he has arrived at some of the same conclusions that the Soviet scientists have. Not interested in becoming a scientific specimen, Mrs. Stanley has agreed to aid Youtz's experiments in the hope that the research will some day be able to give added light sensitivity to the blind. It is to her credit that she allows Youtz to observe her talents, since she must divide her time between his research projects and her four children, a husband, pets, and two jobs.

Dr. Youtz has devised several tests which give some indication of the conditions that affect Mrs. Stanley's ability to detect light with her finger tips. When Mrs. Stanley's accuracy fell to half its normal frequency in the face of *New York Times* reporters, Dr. Youtz was at a loss to explain her failure. The month was January and, shortly after the test, Youtz tested the hypothesis that the temperature and the humidity of the air surrounding Mrs. Stanley had affected her ability. He turned up the thermostat and boiled water on the stove until he had brought the temperature to 80 degrees and the humidity to 50 per cent. In those conditions, Mrs. Stanley's ability regained its normal accuracy and, in fact, was the highest for the entire month of January 1964.

Dr. Youtz has attempted to explain the effect of the temperature and humidity change in terms of the blood vessels which are near the surface of the skin. In warm weather, there are more vessels near the surface of the skin than in cold. Dr. Youtz thinks that the light receptors which are within the skin are more sensitive under these conditions.

It took much talking, but Dr. Youtz was able to convince a colleague, Dr. Donald E. DeGraaf, to visit with Mrs. Stanley. Protesting that such investigations were all "nonsense," the associate professor of physics at Flint College of the University of Michigan went away from the Stanley house convinced that what he had observed was not a hoax at all, but a genuine phenomenon that was worthy of investigation.

Dr. DeGraaf's explanation, which he cautions is very tentative, fits with Youtz's. He feels that the radiation that is being detected is electromagnetic in character, which sparks off a photochemical process, which in turn relays an impulse to the brain. The most important unknown is the nature of the receptors, which are sensitive to light and relay the signal to the brain.

While orthodox scientists are busy discovering Extra Ocular Vision, the files of "psi" researchers have long contained accounts of people who were able to "see" without the use of their eyes.

The first white men who visited the Samoan Islands witnessed several demonstrations in which blind natives were able to detect visual sensations without the use of their eyes.

An Italian investigator, Dr. Jules Romain, detected this ability in several people and did extensive work trying to determine the exact nature of the phenomenon. All he got for his efforts were a number of interesting case studies and a collection of jibes from his scientific colleagues. His experimentation ended in 1924, and the official view of the scientific establishment at the time was that his work was not orthodox in nature and that it had not been complete.

Dr. Cesare Lombroso, famed Italian physician and criminologist, described an experience he had with a girl who went blind, then developed the ability to see with the tip of her nose and the lobe of her left ear!

Perhaps the most famous case of a person possessing Extra Ocular Vision is that of Miss Mollie Fancher of New York City. When she was a child, this woman sustained injuries which not only made her blind, but an invalid as well. Her case was investigated by Judge Abram H. Daily who eventually wrote a book describing his experiences with Miss Fancher. It is probably the most well documented account of EOV in existence today. Hundreds of people were able to witness Mollie Fancher as she performed. Several physicians certified that she was completely blind, yet she was able to relate the contents of letters and newspapers by running her fingers over the tops of them.

When asked how she was able to see, Mollie replied that she saw with "the back of her head." She could do expert needle work, which she found easier to manage when she held the piece above her head in a strong light.

It would be convenient, from the scientist's point of view, if these were the limits of EOV. Without any added challenging facts, the position now fits neatly into some branches of biology and physics. But facts pay no heed to theories, and orthodox scientists on both sides of the Atlantic are finding too many facts for present scientific theory to handle.

Mollie Fancher is a particularly disturbing case, for this remarkably gifted woman did not always require the use of her skin for the detection of images. At one time she was with a group of people at her home and a letter came for one of those present. Before it had been opened she related the entire contents to the group. She could read newspapers without bothering to unroll them—a simple matter of running her fingers over the wrapper and then relating the contents to a friend, who then could read it for himself if he desired to open the paper and hunt for the articles on the center pages. Exactly what kind of light receptors are able to pierce opaque pieces of paper are not known to man.

Mollie Fancher also claimed that she was able to look around the city at times. Once she described a man whom she had never met to Judge Daily, claiming she had seen the man at the Judge's house. The Judge was astounded, because she had described the visitor perfectly.

Soviet Russia's push to understand EOV has lead it to a series of amazing discoveries. Rosa Kuleshova, who, with practice, has been able to extend her ability to reading sentences and music as well as separating colors with the tips of her fingers, has, in addition, developed the power to merely touch the topmost piece of material in a pile, then call off the color of each succeeding piece of material without letting her hand leave the top.

Even though Rosa cannot see with her hands when the room is darkened, most of the people who possess Extra Ocular Vision are able to detect colors and figures in the darkest surroundings. In such a situation, electromagnetic radiation in the visible range is not being reflected from objects, which makes them invisible to the eyes and all other light-sensing apparatus. Yet Nadia Lobanova, a Russian girl of ten, who has been blind since she was one, is able to read big letters and detect colors in such a setting.

Soviet and American researchers have tested the hypothesis that the colors and figures have been delivered telepathically from the observers to the subject. But Rosa Kuleshova is able to take a book, open it to a random page while blindfolded, and identify words or sentences on the page when no observers are present. This can then be checked, and each time the girl has tried, she has been able to read the first words of a random page correctly. Thus it does not seem possible that telepathic signals disclose the colors or the words.

These sensitive people do not describe colors with the same words that usually accompany visual sensations. Rosa Kuleshova, for example, describes white as smooth, and black as "peas under my fingers." Red is a zig zag line, while green comes to her in little squares. Others have termed colors hot or cold, slippery, or a "series of little lines." Whatever the acceptable explanation will finally be, it will have to encompass considerably more facts than the tentative hypotheses do. Until such an explanation can be formulated, "psi" investigators can only hope that this inroad of the orthodox will lend credence to the entire effort of parapsychology.

8.

ASTRAL PROJECTION AND
HUMAN DOUBLES

On July 8, 1896, a perplexed William MacDonald sat in a New York City courtroom and heard himself formally accused of attempting to burglarize a house on Second Avenue. According to several witnesses, MacDonald had been discovered bumping about in a room, apparently trying to make off with valuable items. The witnesses had tried to grab him, but MacDonald had somehow managed to escape. All the witnesses testified, however, that they had had opportunity for a good look at him.

When the puzzled MacDonald had been arrested by the police and had been taken before the witnesses, they were unanimous in swearing that he was definitely the man they had seen in the house on Second Avenue.

Although MacDonald could offer little by way of alibi without the testimony of a certain corroborating witness, his defense attorney found that this key witness was most willing to appear on the accused man's behalf. This witness was Professor Wein, a noted New York hypnotist, who enjoyed a good reputation in the world of conventional scientific medicine.

"On the very hour in which Mr. MacDonald is accused of attempting to burgle the house on Second Avenue," Professor Wein told an astonished courtroom, "he was in reality on the stage of a Brooklyn vaudeville house, which is more than five miles away from the aforementioned house. What is more, Mr. MacDonald was under the close scrutiny of an audience of several hundred people. You see, he was assisting me in my performance, and I had placed him in a deep hypnotic trance."

The judge frowned, rapped his gavel for silence as excited murmurs arose from spectators in the courtroom. The prosecuting attorney seemed stunned by such a pronouncement.

With the permission of the court, the defense attorney called ten reputable Brooklyn residents before the judge's bench. Professor Wein explained that these men and women had served as a committee on the stage while he was performing. It had been their function to see that his claims for hypnosis were not implemented by any sort of trickery. Now, the members of the committee could serve quite another purpose: they could identify William MacDonald as the man Professor Wein had placed in a deep trance.

The prosecuting attorney sat very still for a few moments after the defense attorney had indicated that he might cross-examine the witness. He had walked into the courtroom with what had seemed like an open and shut case. Now, in a most incredible way, his task had been made much more difficult.

"Professor Wein," he asked the witness, "do you mean to tell the court that it was possible for Mr. MacDonald to be in two places at the same time?"

"The physical Mr. MacDonald never left the stage of the Brooklyn vaudeville house," the professor told the attorney. "It may have been a non-physical image of Mr. MacDonald that the residents at the house on Second Avenue saw."

"Do you mean," the prosecutor pressed on, "that it was possible for Mr. MacDonald's spirit to wander while his physical body was on the stage of the theater?"

"Yes," Professor Wein nodded. "This is quite possible."

Once again the judge had to sound his gavel for silence in the courtroom.

The prosecutor scratched his chin reflectively, continued his cross-examination. "What, Professor Wein, did you suggest that Mr. MacDonald do while under your hypnotic trance?"

"I only placed him in a deep sleep."

"Did you suggest that he go to New York?"

The professor was firm on this point. "No. I neither suggested that he should go to New York, nor did I speak of New York to him. In fact, I did not even think of New York while I had Mr. MacDonald in trance."

"As a part of your performance," the prosecutor asked, "did you command Mr. MacDonald to commit a crime or to act out the perpetration of a crime?"

"Most certainly not!"

The prosecutor paused in his questioning, as if he had expected the defense attorney to object to his line of questioning. No objection came. The defense was allowing Professor Wein's testimony to establish its case and had no fear that the prosecutor might be able to confuse him or trip him up.

"Is Mr. MacDonald a good subject?" he asked, breaking his silence.

"One of the best that I have ever encountered in the course of my experience."

"Does he follow all the commands which you give him?"

Professor Wein paused, thoughtfully considering his answer. "I am convinced that Mr. MacDonald, while in the hypnotic state, would carry out all my suggestions within certain limits. I must stress, however, that I would never suggest that any subject commit or dramatize the perpetration of any criminal act. I consider that my subjects are in cataleptic states and are deprived for a certain time of all sensations other than those which I impose upon them. Such an out-of-the-body experience as that which Mr. MacDonald underwent is not without precedent in the annals of hypnosis."

Although the prosecuting attorney did his best to un-

dermine the professor's testimony by attempting to portray such an experience as fantastic and unbelievable,
the jury returned a verdict of "not guilty." For the first
time, a New York jury placed credence in a case of
"psi" phenomena and acquitted a man because he literally had been in two places at one time.

The strange phenomenon of astral projection, or bilo-
cation, is another aspect of "psi" which does peculiar
things to the conventional concept of a three-dimensional world and the space-time continuum. Although many
people regard the ability to project one's "astral self"
as something lifted directly from a science-fiction writer's imagination, the phenomenon—like all aspects of
"psi"—has been noted for centuries.

On October 25, 1593, a strange soldier suddenly appeared among the sentries on guard in front of the palace
in Mexico City. The bewildered man stared around him
as if he were in a dream. The soldiers on guard duty
could certainly commiserate with him, because they were
just as baffled as he. One moment they had been chat-
ting idly before the palace, the next, a strange soldier
had appeared in their midst dressed in the uniform of a
guard for the Governor's Palace in the capital of the
Philippines!

"My name is Gil Perez," he told the men who chal-
lenged him. "This morning I was ordered to stand
guard at the doors of the Governor's Palace in Manila.
I know that this is not Manila, but this is a palace of
some kind, so I am doing my duty as well as I can."

When astonished guards told Perez that he was in
Mexico City, thousands of miles away from Manila, the
man could not believe it. Neither could the Holy Office. All the man's identification indicated that he had indeed "left" Manila that morning and had accomplished
a several-thousand-mile trip in a matter of moments. The
clergy quickly had Perez jailed as an agent of the Devil
and began at once to attempt to shake his testimony.

Two months later a galleon arrived from the Philippines. Fortunately for the hapless Perez, the galleon had among its passengers an official of the court in Manila, who recognized him as a palace guard and testified that he had seen the man shortly before he embarked for Mexico on official business.

Confronted with such testimony on the part of such an eminent witness, the Holy Office decided that Perez had been an innocent victim of the Devil and allowed him to return by ship to the Philippines.

In 1774, while in prison at Arezzo, Italy, Alfonso de Liguori awakened one morning and proclaimed that he had been at the bedside of the dying Pope Clement XIV. The prisoner was laughed at and mocked and his delusion was attributed to a fast that he had imposed upon himself. Subsequent investigation, however, revealed that those present at the Pope's bedside had actually seen Alfonso de Liguori standing among them.

Often such "out-of-the-body" experiences are encountered by individuals who have come close to death. Whether or not such experiences prove survival beyond the grave is a matter of individual interpretation. Such cases are striking and quite provocative and most have the similarity of mentioning a "silver cord" that connects the free floating "astral" self to the physical body. A case from Volume viii of the *Proceedings* of the Society for Psychical Research offers an illustration worth examination.

A Dr. Wiltse of Skiddy, Kansas, felt himself to be dying and bade good-bye to his family and friends. Dr. S. M. Raynes, the attendant physician, said that Dr. Wiltse passed four hours without pulse or perceptible heart-beat. The doctor said he thought he perceived an occasional very slight gasp.

Dr. Wiltse, meanwhile, had regained a state of "conscious existence" and discovered that he no longer had anything in common with his body. In this new state of consciousness, he began to rock to and fro, trying to break connection with the body's tissues. He seemed to "feel and hear the snapping of innumerable small cords," and began to retreat from his feet toward his head "as a rubber cord shortens."

At last he "felt" himself in the head, emerging through the sutures of the skull. "I recollect distinctly," Wiltse said, "how I appeared to myself something like a jellyfish as regards color and form . . . As I emerged from the head, I floated up and down and laterally like a soap bubble attached to the bowl of a pipe until I at last broke loose from the body and fell lightly to the floor, where I slowly rose and expanded into the full stature of a man. I seemed to be translucent, of a bluish cast and perfectly naked."

Wiltse decided that he should exit at once and headed directly for the door. When he got there, he found himself suddenly clothed. Two of his friends stood soberly before the door and were completely oblivious to his presence. To Wiltse's surprise, he found that he passed through them and out of the door.

"I never saw the street more distinctly than I saw it then," he recalled. It was also at this point that Wiltse noticed that he was attached "by means of a small cord, like a spider's web" to his body in the house. Then, as if magically propelled, Wiltse soared into the air and found himself surveying various locales and scenery.

At last he found himself on a road that had steep rocks blocking his journey. He tried to climb around them, but at that moment, "a black cloud descended on me and I opened my eyes to find myself back on my sick bed."

In an address before the Royal Society of Medicine on February 26, 1927, Sir Auckland Geddes told of an out-of-the-body experience that had occurred to him one midnight when he had suddenly begun to feel very ill.

By two o'clock, it was obvious that he was suffering from acute gastroenteritis. By morning his pulse and respiration were too faint for him to count. He wanted to ring for help, but found that he was unable to do so. He concluded that he was dying and "quite placidly gave up the attempt" to summon assistance.

He was then aware that his ego seemed to be separating from another consciousness that was also his. "Gradually," Sir Auckland said in his address, "I realized that I could see not only my body, and the bed it was in, but everything in the whole house and garden, and then I realized that I was seeing not only 'things' at home, but in London and in Scotland, in fact wherever my attention was directed . . . I was free in a time-dimension of space, where 'now' was in some way equivalent to 'here' in the ordinary three-dimensional space of everyday life."

Sir Auckland then told of seeing someone enter his bedroom, regard his appearance with shock, and summon a doctor with the words, "He is nearly gone!" The physician came and injected camphor into his veins.

"As the heart began to beat more strongly, I was drawn back, and I was intensely annoyed, because I was so interested and just beginning to understand where I was and what I was 'seeing.' I came back into the body really angry at being pulled back, and once I was back, all the clarity of vision of anything and everything disappeared and I was just possessed of a glimmer of consciousness, which was suffused with pain."

The Reverend L. J. Bertrand, a Huguenot minister, while on a holiday in the Alps, found himself drifting into the "sleep of the snows" after he had sat down to await the arrival of his guide and a number of students, who had accompanied him on a mountain climbing expedition.

Reverend Bertrand felt his body gradually becoming immovable and realized with a start that he had sat still too long and was freezing to death. There was a violent burst of pain, which he interpreted as the act of death, then he suddenly found himself bobbing above his physical body like a balloon on a silver string.

He thought of his students, and his "mind" was suddenly with them, watching them make wrong turns, observing their amateurish climbing methods. Piqued, Bertrand watched the guide retreat behind a rock to eat the lunch he was supposed to have brought up the mountain for the Reverend.

His thoughts were then of his wife, who was to join him in Lucerne three days later. He was surprised to see her arriving ahead of schedule in a carriage with four others.

At about the time he was observing his wife checking into the hotel, the students and the guide came upon his frozen body. At once the guide began to rub his body with snow, and—experiencing the same sort of reluctance which Sir Auckland Geddes had felt—Reverend Bertrand came to himself.

No sooner had he regained consciousness than he began to berate his students for not following his instructions and for not taking the correct turns. Leaving them stunned and frightened, he turned his attention to the guide and belabored him for nibbling at his lunch. The superstitious guide was ready to flee instantly from the man "who sees everything." Bertrand's wife was more than a little disconcerted as well, when her husband later described the carriage in which she had arrived and the other four members of her traveling party. Reverend Bertrand declared that he had at last found personal proof for that which he had been preaching all of his life.

The *Journal* of the Society for Psychical Research, Volume 34, carried the case of an armored-car officer, who, on August 23, 1944, received a direct hit from a German anti-tank gun. The car, which had been filled with explosives, blew up. The force of the explosion threw the officer about twenty-five feet away from the car and over a five-foot hedge.

According to the officer: "I was conscious of being two persons—one, lying on the ground in a field where I had fallen from the blast, my clothes on fire, waving my limbs about wildly, at the same time uttering moans and gibbering with fear. The other 'me' was floating up in the air, about twenty feet from the ground, from which position I could see not only my other self on the ground, but also the hedge, the road, and the car, which was surrounded by smoke and burning fiercely. I remember quite distinctly telling myself, 'It's no use gibbering like that—roll over and over to put the flames out.' This my ground body eventually did, rolling over into a ditch under the hedge where there was a slight amount of water. The flames went out, and at this stage I suddenly became one person again.

"Of course, the aerial viewpoint can be explained up to a point as a 'photograph' taken subconsciously as I was passing over the hedge as a result of the blast. This, however, does not explain the fact that I saw 'myself' on the ground quite clearly and for what seemed a long time, though it could not have been more than a minute or so."

Although these cases deal with the inadvertent projection of an "astral" self, occurring during acute illness or danger, a great many people have exercised this peculiar function of the transcendent self to the extent that they can project their "phantoms" at will.

The famous early "psi" researcher, Edmund Gurney, told of the incredible experiments of a Mr. S. H. Beard in his *Phantasms of the Living,* published in 1886.

Beard began his experiments with "astral projection" in November of 1881 on a Sunday evening after he had been reading of "the great power which the human will is capable of exercising." Exerting the "whole force" of his being on the thought that he would be present "in spirit on the second floor of a house at 22, Hogarth Road, Kensington, England, Beard managed to project a "phantom" that was visible to his fiancee, Miss L. S. Verity.

Three days later, when Beard went to call upon Miss

Verity, a very excited young woman told him that she and her eleven-year-old sister had nearly been frightened out of their wits by an apparition that had looked just like him. Beard felt quite pleased with the success of his experiment. Miss Verity's sister confirmed his "phantom's" appearance, in fact the whole matter of a spectral visitation had been brought up without any allusion to the subject on Beard's part.

Miss Verity later told Edmund Gurney that she "distinctly saw Mr. Beard in my room, about one o'clock. I was perfectly awake and was much terrified. I awoke my sister by screaming, and she saw the apparition herself. Neither my sister nor I have ever experienced hallucinations of any sort."

Although Beard did not disclose his intentions to Miss Verity, he was by no means finished with his experimentations. The second time he was seen by a married sister of Miss Verity's, whom he had met briefly only once before. Beard walked up to the bed on which the sister lay, took her long hair into his hand, and, a bit later, took her hand into his.

When investigator Gurney learned of Beard's second successful projection, he wrote him a note and urged him to let him know the next time that he planned to experiment. Beard complied, and, in a letter dated March 22, 1884, he told the "psi" researcher simply, "This is it."

Gurney next heard from Beard on April 3rd. A statement from Miss Verity was enclosed:

"On Saturday night, March 22nd . . . at about midnight, I had a distinct impression that Mr. S. H. B. was present in my room, and I distinctly saw him whilst I was widely awake. He came towards me and stroked my hair . . . The appearance in my room was most vivid and quite unmistakable."

Again, Miss Verity testified that she had voluntarily given Mr. Beard the information without any prompting on his part. Mr. Beard concluded his experiments after this episode for Miss Verity's nerves "had been much shaken, and she had been obliged to send for a doctor in the morning."

A paper entitled "On the Evidence for Clairvoyance" by Mrs. Henry Sidgwick, which appeared in Volume vii of the *Proceedings* of the Society for Psychical Research, includes a vivid example of an out-of-the-body experience that was hypnotically produced.

A woman named Jane was put into hypnotic trance by a Dr. F., who was experimenting with "traveling clairvoyance." The doctor had arranged to have one of his patients, a Mr. Eglinton, sit in his apartment that night so that Jane might clairvoyantly come calling on him. Jane had never met Mr. Eglinton, who was thin and weak after a bout with a serious illness, nor had she ever been to the district in which he lived.

After she had been placed in trance, Jane was told to "travel" to Mr. Eglinton's apartment. She accurately described the approach to the house, the knocker on the door, and the furnishings in the room. But when she described the appearance of Mr. Eglinton, Dr. F. felt that the experiment had failed. According to Jane's description, Mr. Eglinton was fat and had an artificial leg.

Dr. F. recalled Jane, puzzled that she should go so far astray on the appearance of the man when she had described everything else so exactly. It was not until the next day that he discovered that Mr. Eglinton had grown weary with waiting up for the experiment and had fashioned a dummy of himself to maintain a vigil in the sitting room. He had stuffed his clothes with several pillows and had propped the mannikin up beside a glass of brandy and some newspapers. Hence, the "Mr. Eglinton" Jane had seen in the apartment had indeed been fat and possessed of artificial limbs.

The American novelist, Theodore Dreiser, often told of the night in which he had entertained the English writer, John Cowper Powys. The Englishman had had to leave rather early and both men expressed regret that their evening had been so short.

Seeing that Dreiser's concern was genuine, Powys told him: "I'll appear before you, right here, later this evening. You'll see me."

"Will you turn yourself into a ghost?" Dreiser asked, chuckling at the Englishman's peculiar sense of humor.

"I'm not certain yet," Powys told him. "I may return as a spirit or in some other astral form."

Several hours later, as Dreiser sat reading in his easy chair, he glanced up and was startled to see Powys standing before him, looking exactly as he had appeared earlier that evening. When the writer moved toward the apparition and spoke to it, the astral projection of Powys disappeared.

Sylvan J. Muldoon is one of those who claim that astral projection can be learned, developed, and mastered by the serious-minded. In his two books, *The Projection of the Astral Body* (1929) and *The Case for Astral Projection* (1936), Muldoon offers a detailed record of many experiments he has personally conducted, and provides a systematic method of inducing the conditions necessary for astral projection. According to Muldoon, it is possible to leave the body at will and retain full consciousness in the "astral self." Muldoon is also cognizant of the "silver cord," mentioned earlier as connecting the phantom body and the physical body. This cord, says Muldoon, is extremely elastic and permits a journey of considerable distance. Muldoon claims to have been able to move objects while in his astral self and to have gained information that he could not have acquired via any of the normal sensory channels.

Muldoon is generous in providing the reader with copious descriptions of the mechanism of astral projection in order that the truly interested student can follow the procedures and attempt his own experimentation. The fundamental law of projection, according to Muldoon, is expressed in these words: "When the subconscious will becomes possessed of the idea to move the body, and the physical body is incapacitated, the subconscious will moves the astral body out of the physical."

Frederic W. H. Myers has written that cases of astral projection present perhaps not the most useful, "but the most extraordinary achievement of the human will. What can lie further outside any known capacity than the power to cause a semblance of oneself to appear at a distance? What can be more a central action—more manifestly the outcome of whatsoever is deepest and most unitary in man's whole being? Of all vital phenomena, I say, this is the most significant; this self-projection is the one definite act which it seems as though a man might perform equally well before and after bodily death."

Another phenomenon, which must be closely related to the projection of the astral self, is that of the appearance of one's own double.

The Archbishop Frederic wrote to Sir Oliver Lodge in 1929 to tell him of a most peculiar incident which had occurred on the evening of January 14th. He had returned to his home feeling very tired, sat down in a favorite easy chair, and immediately fell asleep.

"I was sharply aroused," he wrote in the letter, "in about a quarter of an hour (as I perceived by the clock). As I awoke I saw an apparition, luminous, vaporous, wonderfully real of myself, looking interestedly and delightedly at myself. Some books lying on a table back of my ghost I could see and identify.

"After I and myself had looked at each other for the space of about five seconds, my ghostly self vanished for a few seconds, only to return in a more definitely clear way . . ."

Goethe, the great German poet, had the astonishing experience of meeting himself as he rode away from

Frederika at Strassburg. The phantom wore a dress—pike grey with gold lace—which Goethe had never seen before. Eight years later, as Goethe was on the same road going to visit Frederika, it occurred to him that he was dressed in precisely the same dress that his phantom had been wearing on that earlier occasion.

Such weird phenomena are termed *autoscopic hallucinations*. They serve no dual purpose, such as providing a warning or disclosing valuable information, but only seem to present a projection of one's own body image. One sees oneself, as it were, without a mirror.

In the April, 1966, issue of *Fate,* Dr. Edward Podolsky has compiled a number of cases of people who have reported seeing their own ghosts, in an article entitled "Have You Seen Your Double?"

Dr. Podolsky records the experience of a Mr. Harold C. of Chicago, Illinois, who, in March, 1958, returned home after a hard day at the office with a splitting migraine. As he sat down to dinner, he saw, sitting opposite him, an exact replica of himself. This astonishing double repeated every movement he made during the entire course of the meal. Since that time, Mr. C. has seen his double on a number of occasions—each time after an attack of migraine.

Samuel V. of Kansas City, Missouri, was startled to see an exact double of himself duplicating his every movement as he went about gardening chores. The double was visible for about two hours.

Most frightening is the case of Mrs. Jeanie P. As she was applying makeup, she saw an exact duplicate of herself also touching up *her* features. Mrs. P. reached out to touch the double, and the image reached out to touch her. Mrs. P. actually felt her face being touched by her mysterious double.

According to Dr. Podolsky, there are two main theories about the cause of autoscopy. One theory regards the phenomenon as being due to "the result of some irritating process in the brain, particularly of the parietotemporal-occipital area (the visual area)." The other, a psychological theory, sees in autoscopy "the projection of memory pictures. Certain pictures are stored in the memory and when conditions of stress or other unusual psychological situations arise these memories may be projected outside the body as very real images."

Neither theory explains the "Vardogr" of the Norwegians. Wiers Jensen, editor of the *Norwegian Journal of Psychical Research,* wrote a series of articles on the Vardogr as early as 1917. The possessor of a Vardogr unconsciously employs it as a type of spiritual forerunner to announce his physical arrival.

"The Vardogr reports are all alike," wrote Wiers Jensen. "With little variation, the same type of happening occurs: The possessor of a Vardogr *announces* his arrival. His steps are heard on the staircase. He is heard to unlock the outside door, kick off his overshoes, put his walking stick in place, etc. The listening 'percipients' —if they are not so accustomed to the prelude of the Vardogr that they remain sitting quietly—open the door and find the entry empty. The Vardogr has, as usual, played a trick on them. Eight or ten minutes later, the whole performance is repeated—but now the reality and the man arrive."

Being of Norwegian and Danish descent (it seems that only the Norwegians and the Scotch experience this particular type of "psi" phenomenon), I can relate my personal experiences with the Vardogr.

One Saturday night when I was about sixteen, I managed to arrive home before my parents. I went upstairs to my room and lay down on the bed to thumb through a new magazine I had purchased that evening. I had not lain there long when I heard the front door open and the sounds of my parents moving about downstairs. The sounds had been quite clear. First the opening of the front screen door, then the individual squeaking of the inside door. The sound of footsteps mounting the three steps to the inner hallway had been very audible, as had been the subsequent sounds of footsteps moving about the various rooms.

"Goodnight!" I shouted down the stairs after a few moments.

There was no answer. I flipped through a few more pages of the magazine, thinking that my parents had not heard me as they prepared for bed.

"Goodnight down there!" I shouted after a few moments, a bit louder this time.

Again no answer. And by now it had become very silent downstairs. Too silent if those footsteps had really belonged to my parents. My mind was instantly flooded with a variety of startling images. Burglars, thinking the home deserted and not seeing my light, had decided to enter the house. My shouts had alerted them to the presence of a lone occupant. What would their next move be? Icy fingers traced a slow, deliberate path up the length of my spine.

At the moment I was about to reach for my .22 rifle to do battle, I once again heard the familiar sounds of my parents arriving home. The noises were precisely as they had been before, only this time when I shouted down my "goodnight," the voices of my parents quickly responded.

The second time I heard the Vardogr of my parents was no less eerie, and neither were any of its subsequent arrivals. Each time it tricked me as thoroughly as it had done before. My sister fell victim to its spooky pranks fully as often as I. One night my parents arrived home to find her in a state of near panic. She had been sitting in a chair with her back to the door. She had heard the door open and close and the sound of footsteps enter the house and approach to the spot directly behind her chair. As she was engrossed in the book she was reading, she had not bothered to turn around at the sound of the opening door. After a few moments had passed, she began to wonder why her mother and father preferred to stand behind her chair in complete silence. Imagine her surprise and horror when she turned around and saw that no one was there.

Weirs Jensen, in one of his articles, notes the fact that, as a rule, the Vardogr announces itself only by imitating the sounds made by inanimate objects, such as "the sound of the key in the lock, the placing of overshoes and stick in their proper spots, the stamping of shoes on the floor. The jingle of horsebells and the cracking of whips may also be heard."

At times, though, the Vardogr may materialize into such an independent apparition that it may be mistaken for the real man.

In the summer of 1955, Mr. Erkson Gorique decided to visit Norway to investigate the possibilities of importing Norwegian china and glassware. A successful businessman in his fifties, Mr. Gorique had traveled widely but had never been to Norway. Each summer for several years he had declared his intention of making the trip to the land of fjords and icy streams, but something had always interfered with his plans and the trip had never been accomplished.

In July he landed in Oslo, inquired where he might find the best hotel, and took a taxi directly to the recommended lodgings. He knew absolutely no one in Norway and was prepared to go about his business in no great haste.

When Mr. Gorique registered at the desk, the clerk greeted him with a pleasant smile. "How nice to see you again, Mr. Gorique. It is so good to have you back."

Gorique stared at the man, managed a thin smile. "But I have never been here before. You must mistake me for someone else."

The clerk frowned, shook his head resolutely. "Surely you remember, sir. It has only been a few months since you dropped by one morning to make a reservation and told me that you would be along about this time in the summer."

Gorique could do nothing but blink incredulously.

Uneasy under the importer's peculiar stare, the clerk stammered. "Well, sir, that is, well, your name is a bit unusual. That's why I was able to remember it."

"This just cannot be!" Gorique said firmly. "I have never been to Oslo nor to Norway in my entire life!"

Mr. Gorique's voice had carried across the lobby and the manager had appeared in the background, narrow-eyed and nervous. The clerk caught a glimpse of the manager out of the corner of his eye and offered a wide smile to the American importer. "I must be mistaken, sir. Please forgive me."

Gorique walked away from the desk with the distinct impression that although the clerk had confessed his error, he thought the American either mad or attempting to travel incognito.

Matters did not improve for Mr. Gorique when he visited the wholesale dealer whom he had planned to see about arranging for the importation of glassware. Mr. Olsen, a white-haired, friendly man, rose from behind his desk and offered the importer his hand in a hearty handclasp. Before Gorique could speak, Olsen exclaimed: "How wonderful that you did get back, Mr. Gorique. You were in such a hurry the last time that we were not able to conclude the final details of our business."

Completely stunned, all the argument sapped from his body, Gorique slumped into a chair in Olsen's office. "Tell me," he said weakly. "When was I here?"

"Why," Olsen answered, looking puzzled, "just a few months back."

With a sigh of resignation, Gorique appealed to the Norwegian glassware dealer. He protested that he had never been to Norway before in his life and that he could prove it; yet everywhere he went, the hotel clerks, the waiters, and now Mr. Olsen, recognized him and spoke of former visits.

Olsen listened to the bewildered man's story without interruption, then told him about the Vardogr.

"I can offer no explanation for the Vardogr," Olsen

told the baffled Mr. Gorique, "but it is really not such a rare thing as psychic phenomena go. You really shouldn't let such an experience disturb you unduly."

Perhaps this attitude is not a bad one to hold as one continues to explore deeper into the world of ESP.

9.

FROM THE EDGE OF THE GRAVE

Dr. Augustus Jessopp was in high spirits on that chilly autumn night in 1879. Lord Orford had invited him to spend the night at Mannington Hall and had given him permission to examine some very old books in his extensive library.

Although Dr. Jessopp enjoyed the animated conversation with the other guests, he could hardly wait until the others had gone to bed so that he could begin taking notes from the old books in the library. A dentist by profession, Dr. Jessopp was an antiquarian by hobby.

At last, by eleven o'clock, Lord Orford and his other guests had retired for the evening, and Dr. Jessopp was alone in the library with all the treasured volumes. He set immediately to work, taking notes from six small books. He had four large candles on his desk and a crackling fire in the fireplace. The light was excellent. Exhilarated from an evening of stimulating and delightful companionship, he felt as though he could work through the night.

At 1:30 A.M., Dr. Jessopp glimpsed something white about a foot from his left elbow. Upon closer examination, the object proved to be a large, extremely pale hand with dark blue veins across its back.

Putting his pen aside, Dr. Jessopp turned and saw that he shared the desk with a tall, solidly built man, who seemed to be intent upon examining both the dentist and the books he had been studying. The strange visitor had a lean, rugged profile and reddish-brown hair, which had been closely cut. He was dressed in a black habit of the type worn by clergymen in the early 1800's, and he sat in a posture of complete relaxation with hands clasped lightly together. After a few moments, Dr. Jessop realized that the man was not staring at him at all; rather, the stranger seemed completely unaware of his presence.

Dr. Jessopp had not for one moment considered his late evening visitor to be anything other than a living person, but he did think it most peculiar that he had not met the clergyman earlier in the evening and a bit strange that the man would enter the room and seat himself so silently at the same desk. It was not until the man vanished before his eyes that Dr. Jessopp realized he had been visited by a ghost.

Dr. Jessopp was a very stolid sort of individual, not easily frightened or easily impressed by anything out of the ordinary. His most pronounced reaction was one of disappointment, because he had not had time to make a sketch of the ghostly clergyman.

He had returned to his note-taking and was perhaps wondering how he could sensibly relate the story of his spectral visitor to Lord Orford when he once again saw the white hands appear next to his own. The figure sat in precisely the same position as before and the expression on his face had not changed the slightest. The ghostly clergyman still seemed to sit, hands folded, in an attitude of contemplation or complete relaxation.

Dr. Jessopp turned to give the ghost his full attention. It had occurred to him that he might speak to the specter, and he had begun to form a sentence in his mind. He wanted it to be just the kind of provocative statement that would prompt a ghost to utter a response. Then, before his lips could form the sentence and give it utterance, he seemed suddenly to fully realize the eeriness of the whole situation. A sense of deep dread and fear began to permeate his entire being. An unconscious reflex knocked a book to the desk, and the ghost vanished instantly at the harsh sound.

The story of Dr. Jessopp's ghost became so exaggerated in the telling and re-telling by others, that the dentist allowed the *London Athenaeum* to print an authorized account of the incident about two months after the uncanny experience.

Dr. Jessopp emphasized in the article that he was not in the habit of engaging in flights of fancy and did not wish to be "looked upon as a kind of medium to whom supernatural visitations are vouchsafed . . . or a crazy dreamer whose disorganized nervous system renders him abnormally liable to fantastic delusions." The dentist also stressed the point that he had been in perfect health on the night of the visitation and had been in no way approaching weariness or fatigue. He also stated that the talk at Mannington Hall that evening had concerned itself with travel and art and had in no way touched upon the supernatural. The ghost, he added, did not appear wispy or cloaked in a traditional sheet. The figure appeared lifelike, natural, and so solid that it had blocked the light from the fireplace.

After the aforementioned experience, there was no question in Dr. Jessopp's mind—as there is none in mine —that "ghosts" do exist. But the ghosts, which we might suddenly encounter some night on the stairs or in a hotel room where we have elected to spend the night, differ in many respects from the portrayals of ghosts in horror films and stories. These differences will be noted in the examples that follow.

Early in 1950, Ted Henty, an ex-cop from Brighton, England, formed his own group of professional "ghost hunters." These men arm themselves with dozens of microphones, six cameras of conventional design, an infrared camera, four wire recorders, an electric eye hookup and several other scientific "ghost catchers." Most of the homes which the crew "de-ghost" have been found to be haunted by pigeons, mice, tree branches, and over-active imaginations. Henty shall be forever forced to keep an open mind, however, because of an experience that occurred to him when his crew was summoned by an estate owner who could not keep servants because of the visitation of the ghost of a female Indian.

Henty interviewed the domestics, who had resigned their positions because of the ghost, and gained their descriptions of the unwelcome specter. He learned that it had been a harsh economic strain for two of the maids to quit, yet they had resigned out of fear of something which they could not understand. Henty arrived at the home to make a preliminary investigation and to plan camera and microphone positions.

Then: "There it was! What looked unmistakably like the blurred figure of a dark-skinned lady dressed in white, somewhat smallish, smiling, walking toward me. I was stunned. The very thing I had always argued against seemed to be approaching, and I could see it in fairly clear light with my own two eyes. I had no camera with me then and so all I could do was stand there, open-mouthed, until this thing went through an open door into a large bedroom and disappeared without a trace."

Later that night, one of Henty's cameramen got an image on film of a small, vaguely defined figure dressed in white. The face was darkly Indian. Each member of Henty's twelve-man crew swears that the film had not been tampered with in any way.

Shortly before Easter in 1964, several parishioners and a caretaker were cleaning St. Columbkille's Roman Catholic Church in Uptergrove, Ontario, Canada, in preparation for the holiday services. To their collective amazement, they saw a shadowy figure wearing a black choir gown glide over to the organ, sit down, and begin to play. When two members of the party approached the phantom, it entered a room leading to the belfry. A carpenter made a grab for the phantom, but his hands "just seemed to come together in thin air."

In 1882 the first major undertaking of the newly formed Society for Psychical Research was to conduct a Census of Hallucinations by means of a circulated questionnaire:

Have you ever, when believing yourself to be completely awake, had a vivid impression of seeing or being touched by a living being or inanimate object, or of hearing a voice; which impression, so far as you could discover, was not due to any external physical cause?

The SPR received answers from 17,000 people, 1,684 of whom answered "yes." From this, the committee which was conducting the census estimated that nearly 10 per cent of the population had experienced some kind of visual or auditory "hallucination." Those people who indicated that they had experienced some paranormal appearance or manifestation were sent forms requesting details.

The Census of Hallucinations enabled the early researchers to arrive at a number of basic premises concerning ghosts and apparitions, which were strengthened by subsequent research. The committee was able to conclude, for example, that although apparitions are connected with other events besides death, they are more likely to be linked with death than with anything else. Visual hallucinations were the most common (1,087). (This is important to note because psychologists tell us that auditory experiences are the most common among the mentally ill.) Of the visual cases reported, 283 had been shared by more than one percipient (also of great importance because critics of psychic phenomena have always argued that the appearance of a "ghost" is an entirely subjective experience). Those who answered the second form indicated that they had not been ill when they had seen their hallucinations and insisted that the hallucinations were quite unlike the bizarre, nightmarish creatures which might appear during high fevers or high alcoholic consumptions. Of the 493 reported auditory hallucinations, 94 had occurred when another person had been present. Therefore, about one-third of the cases were collective, that is, experienced by more than one percipient at the same time.

After the findings of the Census of Hallucinations were made public, the SPR began to be flooded by personal accounts of spontaneous cases of ghosts and apparitions. In order to aid an appointed committee in the handling of such an influx of material, the SPR worked out a series of questions that could be applied to each case that came in.

1. Is the account first hand?
2. Was it written or told before the corresponding event was known?
3. Has the principal witness been corroborated?
4. Was the percipient awake at the time?
5. Was the percipient an educated person of good character?
6. Was the apparition recognized?
7. Was it seen out of doors?
8. Was the percipient anxious or in a state of expectancy?
9. Could relevant details have been read back into the narrative after the event?
10. Could the coincidence between the experience and the event be accounted for by chance?

Later, J. Fraser Nicol established three points of critique that could be used by the investigator of spontaneous phenomena.

1. That the experience be veridical, i.e., that it relate to an actual event that was occurring, had occurred, or would occur.
2. That there be an independent witness who testifies that the percipient related his experience to him before he came to know, by normal means, that the experience had been veridical, and

3. That no more than five years have passed between the experience and the written account of it.

There occurs in the *Proceedings* of the Society for Psychical Research, Volume vi, a case that has always struck me as being an especially good example of the sort of veridical experience that has a great deal of value for "psi" researchers.

In 1876, Mr. F. G., a traveling salesman, was sitting in a hotel room in St. Joseph, Missouri. It was high noon, and Mr. F. G. was smoking a cigar, and writing out orders. Suddenly conscious of someone sitting on his left with one arm resting on the table, the salesman was startled to look up into the face of his dead sister.

"So sure was I that it was she," he said later, "that I sprang forward in delight, calling her by name."

As he did so, the apparition vanished. (To define terms a bit: in the jargon of parapsychology, a *ghost* is usually a stranger to the percipient; while an *apparition* is well known, instantly recognizable to the percipient, usually appears at some time of crisis and usually only once; a *vision* is the appearance of a religious figure, such as the Virgin Mary, an angel, or one of the saints.)

Mr. F. G. resumed his seat, stunned by the experience. The cigar was still in his mouth, the pen was still in his hand, the ink was still moist on his order blank. He was satisfied that he had not been dreaming, but was wide awake.

"She appeared as if alive. Her eyes looked kindly and perfectly naturally into mine. Her skin was so lifelike that I could see the glow of moisture on its surface. . ." Mr. F. G. observed. Then, so impressed was he, that he took the next train home to tell his parents about the remarkable visitation.

Mr. F. G.'s mother nearly fainted when he told them "of a bright red line or scratch on the right-hand side of my sister's face, which I distinctly had seen."

With tears streaming down her face, F. G.'s mother

told him that he had indeed seen his sister, "as no living mortal but herself was aware of that scratch which she had accidentally made while doing some little act of kindness after my sister's death . . . she had carefully obliterated all traces of the slight scratch with the aid of powder . . . and this she had never mentioned to a human being from that day to this."

In *Phantasms of the Living,* Edmund Gurney relates a case that carries a similar denouement.

Gurney's narrator was sitting in his drawing-room with one of his nieces when he saw what appeared to be "dirty soapy water running in at the door." He was about to scold the maid when he realized that the supposed dirty water was the train of a lady's dress. Then, the "lady glided in backwards, as if she had been slid on a slide, each part of her dress keeping its place without disturbance.

"She glided in till I could see the whole of her, except the tip of her nose, her lips and the tip of her chin, which were hidden by the edge of the door."

The strange visitor kept her eyes upon her host and extended her arm, "which was a fine one, in a peculiar way, as if she were proud of it."

The narrator immediately recognized the lady as someone he had known twenty-five years before. They had been good friends and frequent dancing partners, and he remembered her as "a bright, dashing girl." They had not seen one another for more than a quarter of a century, yet the narrator told Gurney that "she looked much as I used to see her—with long curls and bright eyes, but perhaps something stouter and more matronly.

"I said to myself, 'This is one of those strange apparitions I have often heard of. I will watch it as carefully as I can.'"

His niece noticed his strange fascination with the area near the door and exclaimed: "Uncle A., what is the matter with you? You look as if you saw a ghost!"

He motioned her to be quiet and continued to observe the apparition of his old friend.

"I tried to find out whether there was anything in the ornaments on the walls, or anything else which could suggest the figure: but I found all the lines close to her cut the outlines of her figure at all sorts of angles, and none of these coincided with the outline of her figure, and the color of everything around her strongly contrasted with her color."

Uncle A. continued to study the apparition until his brother entered the room and walked "right through the figure," which then began to fade quite rapidly, "first losing the colors and then the form . . ."

It was not until several years later that the percipient learned that his lady friend had died of cancer of the face. "She never showed me the front of her face," he remarked to Gurney. "It was always concealed by the edge of the door."

Not all observers of ghosts and apparitions are able to react as calmly as Uncle A. In the case of the sudden appearance of ghosts in houses that already carry with them a tradition of haunting, the "psychic residue" may provoke feelings of great unease, fear, and extreme panic. Even "psi" researchers are not impervious to such reactions when they are confronted by an especially strong case of negative permeations in a room or locale.

Hereward Carrington, an investigator who had dealt firsthand with mediums, poltergeists, and "haunted houses" on several occasions, found himself reacting to an area of an afflicted house as if he were a complete stranger to things paranormal.

It was on the night of August 13, 1937, that Carrington, his wife, and a party of five others obtained permission to spend the night in a "haunted house," located some fifty miles from New York City. As Carrington referred to the incident in his *Essays in the Occult,* the summer tenant "had been compelled to move back to the city in the middle of July because neither he nor his wife could secure uninterrupted nights of sleep, and . . . their servants had all left in consequence of the haunting."

Carrington insisted that he be told none of the history of the house until he had first had an opportunity to explore the place from cellar to attic. The house was lighted from top to bottom, and the party began its safari into the Unknown.

On the second floor, two or three of the group commented that they had "sensed something strange in one of the middle bedrooms," especially in the area next to an old bureau. The tenant, whom Carrington identified only as "Mr. X," told the party that he and his wife had heard noises coming from that particular bedroom.

They proceeded down a hallway until they came to the door that led to the servant's quarters. Carrington opened the door, glanced up, and saw that the top floor was brightly illuminated and that a steep flight of stairs lay just ahead of the investigators. With Carrington in the lead, the party ascended the stairs until they found themselves confronted by a series of small rooms. Carrington made a sharp turn to the right.

"The instant I did so, I felt as though a vital blow had been delivered to my solar plexus. My forehead broke out into profuse perspiration, my head swam, and I had difficulty in swallowing. It was a most extraordinary sensation, definitely physiological, and unlike anything I had ever experienced before."

The veteran investigator was gripped by terror and panic and only through firm exercise of will was he able to stop himself from fleeing in horror. His wife, who was only a step or two behind him, had just finished commenting on the "cute little rooms," when she suddenly uttered a frightened cry, turned, and ran down the stairs.

Two unemotional, hard-nosed investigators, completely accustomed to psychic manifestations of all kinds, had experienced "distinctly a bodily and emotional reaction—accompanied . . . by a momentary mental panic and sensation of terror" such as neither of them had ever before known.

Carrington saw to his wife, whom he found outside on the porch, breathing deeply of the fresh air, then he returned to the remainder of the party. Each of them had experienced identical sensations and had retreated to the lower floor where they sat sprawled in chairs or leaned against walls, tears streaming down their cheeks. Carrington made special note of the fact that two cynics, friends of the tenant, had accompanied the group out of boredom with their usual entertainments and had brought along a copious supply of Scotch and gin in case they were not confronted with "spirits" of a different nature. Both of these skeptics experienced the same sensations as the other members of the party—a difficulty in swallowing, tears stinging from the eyes, and cold perspiration on the forehead.

A dog, belonging to a member of the party, resisted all manner of coaxing designed to lure it upstairs. It growled, planted its feet stubbornly, and the hair raised on its back. In short, "he behaved very much as dogs are supposed to behave in the presence of ghostly phenomena."

Much later, Carrington led another expedition up the stairs to the servants' quarters. This time, the atmosphere seemed to have purged itself of the poisonous influence, and no member of the party experienced any sensations similar to the previous excursion. The dog bounded up the stairs, poked its nose into all the corners, and behaved as if prowling around such a house were the most natural thing in the world.

Carrington later sought to return to the house with a medium and apparatus for recording and testing sounds and atmosphere. He was denied permission to continue his investigation, because one of the friends of the tenant had given the story to the papers, and the owner of the house did not desire additional publicity about his "haunted house."

One of my favorite "haunted houses" is that manse in Bognor, England, wherein dwelt the shade of the Dark Lady and her indefatigable investigator, Miss Morton. "Miss Morton" was the pseudonym for a young medical student who, when her family moved into the house in April, 1862, discovered that they had acquired a ghost along with the old mansion in Bognor. With a cool emotional detachment, and scientific objectivity, which would be envied by any "psi" researcher, Miss Morton kept following the ghost about, taking notes, conducting tests, and, it seemed, occasionally even frightening the ghost itself.

Miss Morton's family had lived in the house for about two months before the domestics began to complain of footsteps in the hallway at night. Miss Morton described her own first sighting of the Dark Lady, thus: "I had gone to my room but was not yet in bed when I heard someone at the door and went to it, thinking it was my mother. On opening it I saw no one, but going a few steps along the passage I saw the figure of a tall lady, dressed in black, standing at the head of the stairs. After a few moments, she descended the stairs, and I followed for a short distance, curious to see who it was, but I had only a small piece of candle, and it suddenly went out."

Being alone in the dark with a mysterious figure descending the staircase, did not disturb Miss Morton. A maid creaked open a door and told the young mistress that she had seen the Dark Lady on several occasions. Intrigued by the possibilities of having her own ghost, Miss Morton at once decided to study the specter as closely as possible.

"I saw her pass through wires [which she had stretched across the hallway] at least twice," she wrote in her report for the Society for Psychical Research. "I tried to touch her but she always eluded me . . . if I followed her into a corner, she simply disappeared. During the two years, 1882–1884, the only noises I heard were of slight pushes against my bedroom door accompanied by footsteps, and if I looked out, I invariably saw the figure. The footsteps were light. I could hardly hear them except when on linoleum, and then only like someone walking with thin boots on."

The first time that Miss Morton tried to speak to the Dark Lady, she "gave a slight gasp" and moved quickly away from her. The persistent young medical student continued her attempts to engage the ghost in conversation. Once, while passing on the stairs, "she stopped and seemed as if she were about to speak."

Every member of the family and the domestic staff were able to see the Dark Lady except Mr. Morton. On a number of occasions, the father would be led to the spot where the phantom stood, and his impatient family would insist that he should surely be able to see her as well as they. With a gesture of defeat, the father would steadfastly maintain that he could not see their spectral guest. The explanation for Mr. Morton's strange deficiency may have been that the man was simply not sensitive enough or of the proper telepathic affinity to gain a visual image of the Dark Lady.

"Psi" researchers have long recognized four main classes of ghosts and apparitions.

1. Experimental cases in which an agent has deliberately attempted to make his apparitions appear to a particular percipient.

2. "Crisis-apparitions" in which a recognized apparition is seen, heard, or felt when the individual represented by the image is undergoing a crisis, especially death.

3. "Post-mortem apparitions" in which a recognized apparition is seen or heard long after the person represented by the phantom has died.

4. Ghosts or apparitions which habitually appear in a room, house, or locale.

The crisis-apparition of Captain Eldred Bowyer-Bowyer is remarkable because his apparition occurred to more than one person and in widely separated parts of the world.

Captain Bowyer-Bowyer was shot down in his plane in France on March 19, 1917, the same day that he was to be named the godfather of his half-sister's baby. Mrs. Spearman, who was staying in a hotel in Calcutta, India, was fussing with her baby when she suddenly turned around and saw her half-brother standing behind her. Delighted to think that Captain Bowyer-Bowyer had been transferred to India—and just in time to attend the baptismal service—Mrs. Spearman turned back to the bed so that she might set the baby down and embrace her brother. When she once again faced the spot where her brother had stood, she found that he had vanished.

Captain Bowyer-Bowyer had appeared so natural and so lifelike that Mrs. Spearman thought at first that he must be playing a trick on her. She called for him and searched everywhere, then, puzzled, continued on her way to the church. It was not until two weeks later that she read in a newspaper that her half-brother had been shot down on the very day that "he" had appeared in her hotel room.

On the same day, March 19th, Captain Bowyer-Bowyer was also seen by a young niece back in England. At about 9:15 A.M., the girl ran excitedly up to her mother, who was still in bed, and informed her that "Uncle Alley Boy is downstairs!" Her mother smiled and reminded the girl that her uncle was in France, but the excited girl insisted that she had seen "Alley Boy" downstairs.

A third impression of Captain Bowyer-Bowyer was received by a Mrs. Watson, an elderly friend of the airman's mother. On March 19th, she wrote Mrs. Bowyer-Bowyer—to whom she had not written for eighteen months—that she had great feelings of anxiety about Eldred.

A downed aircraft in France, a hotel room in Calcutta, a favorite niece in England, a family friend in yet another locale—time and space mean nothing to the phenomenon of the crisis apparition. Two common features of the crisis apparition are apparent in the case of Captain Eldred Bowyer-Bowyer. One is that the apparition appears so lifelike and so much like the human being it represents that it is almost always mistaken for the actual living person. The other is that crisis-apparitions occur when people least expect them. They suddenly pop up completely unannounced by prior feelings of distress or anxiety about the person whom they represent, and they usually materialize while the percipients are engaged in their normal duties or while they are preparing for sleep.

The Reverend Arthur Bellamy told "psi" researcher F. W. H. Myers about the "lady" he saw one night sitting by the side of the bed where his wife was sound asleep. He stared at the strange woman for several minutes, noting especially the elegant styling of her hair, before the lady vanished.

When Mrs. Bellamy awakened, the reverend described her mysterious caller. He was startled to learn that the description fit that of a schoolgirl friend of his wife's with whom she had once made a pact that the one of them who died first should appear after her death to the survivor.

"But," stammered the astonished Reverend Bellamy, "was there anything outstanding about your friend so that we might be certain?"

"Her hair," his wife replied without hesitation. "We girls used to tease her at school for devoting so much time to the arrangement of her hair."

Later, the clergyman identified a photograph of his wife's friend as being the likeness of the specter that had appeared at her bedside.

G. N. M. Tyrrell saw the ghost or apparition as a "psychological marionette" which is projected by an agent in a time of crisis or great emotion. To Tyrrell, the mechanism of a haunting was similar to an idea, and, at the same time, very much like a pattern. This "idea-pattern" finds sensory expression in the apparition, which has been produced by the dramatic idea of an agent. Tyrrell's "idea-pattern" is distinguished by three general characteristics: "It is dynamic, for it is usually associated with an initiating drive; it is creative, for it manifests an urge towards expression and completeness; and it is tele-ological, for it is marvellously resourceful in adaptation and in adjusting means to ends."

Edmund Gurney theorized that the collective sighting of a ghost is due to a sort of telepathic "infection." One person sees the phantom and in turn telepathically in-fluences another percipient, and so on.

Harry Price developed the "psychic ether" theory of hauntings. In his presidential address to the Society for Psychical Research in 1939, Price hypothesized that a certain level of mind may create a mental image which has a degree of persistence in the psychic ether. This mental image may also contain a telepathic ability by which it can affect other minds. The collective emotions and thought images of a person who has lived in a house for some time may have intensely "charged" the psychic ether of the place—especially if these were powerful emotions such as those of intense hatred or sorrow, or if they had been supercharged by an act of violence. In Price's theory, the original agent has no direct part in the haunting. It is the charged psychic ether which, when presented with a suitable percipient mind of the proper telepathic affinity, co-operates in the production of the idea-pattern of a ghost.

It can be said that every old house, courtroom, hos-pital, castle, railroad depot is "haunted." Any long-in-habited place, which has served as a container for human activity, almost certainly bears existing memory traces; but a multitude of mental images may over-saturate the majority of homes and public places and leave only a mass of impressions which create the peculiar "atmos-phere" so many rooms and locales have. It is only when an idea-pattern that has been charged with enormous psychic intensity finds the mental level of a percipient who has the proper quality of telepathic affinity that a "ghost" can appear.

10.

MEDIUMSHIP AND THE SURVIVAL QUESTION

During November and December of 1908, three distinguished members of the Society for Psychical Research, chaperoned by their secretary, sequestered themselves in the Hotel Victoria in Naples, Italy, with Eusapia Palladino, a well-known medium.

One of the investigators, Mr. Everard Feilding, who had previously stated that he did not believe in paranormal phenomena of *any* kind, later wrote of the sittings in a report for the *Proceedings* of the S.P.R.

According to Feilding, the phenomena of Eusapia Palladino usually began with the levitation of the table around which they sat. "Finally," wrote Feilding, "it would leave the ground entirely and rise to a height of a foot or two rapidly, remain there an appreciable time and then come down."

The most extreme precautions on the part of the investigators would not hinder the medium's powers of levitation in the slightest. She had no hooks on her person or any sort of mechanical device. If the men would press on the table, it would bob up again, as though suspended on some highly elastic material.

"We were constantly touched on the arm, shoulder or head by something which we could not see," Feilding reported. When they were absolutely certain that Eusapia's hands were secured on the table in front of her, the investigators would be grasped "by hands, living hands with fingers and nails."

Once one of these materialized hands seized one of the investigators and nearly tossed him from his chair.

A tea table in a corner of the room rose to shoulder height and set itself in the middle of the seance table.

Tambourines jumped on the researchers' laps; bells lifted themselves from the table and began to ring loudly.

All of these manifestations, and an almost countless number of other phenomena, were accomplished in light adequate enough for the investigators' secretary to take shorthand notes on each astonishing moment with the incredible Eusapia Palladino.

How did the poorly educated woman from Naples accomplish these dramatic manifestations? Was she truly in contact with the spirits of the deceased, or had she learned to harness the energy of an unknown level of the transcendent self? If Eusapia was indeed calling upon the shades of departed and recognizable personalities, if a host of other sincere and honest mediums are truly able to contact the dead, then the survival question has been answered.

But why are we so reluctant to accept the "proofs" of the seance parlor? Is it because we have learned that the human mind is capable of projecting a segment of its psyche unhampered by time and space? Or that one level of the psyche may be able to give "birth" to new personalities? Or that another level of the subconscious may telepathically gain knowledge of the departed from a sitter's mind while yet another level dramatizes that knowledge into an exact imitation of the departed's voice and appearance? It is one of the great paradoxes of "psi" research that the more we have learned about the range and power of the mind, the less credence we tend to give "proof" garnered for the most important question of all: Does man survive death?

Just how important and valuable are the proofs offered us from the seance rooms?

A few years ago, a young editor of a spiritualistic publication wished to present evidence of the spiritist credo that would convince even the most skeptical of the validity of mediumistic phenomena. The young man resolved to photograph several of the most accomplished mediums at work as they met in one of their large summer camps for an annual convention of spiritists. Not wishing to disturb the mediums as they went into trance and produced their ectoplasmic materializations, the journalist snapped his photographs with infra-red flash and special film.

When the photographs were developed, the young editor was shocked to see that the very mediums whose work he had long accepted as genuine were producing their manifestations of the departed by means of trickery. Roll after roll of the film indicated the same disconcerting fact: the mediums at this particular spirtualist camp were all frauds. The editor printed the photographs, and after sweeping up the scattered fragments of his shattered ideal, called for a reform movement in Spiritualism.

No area of human relationships is so open to cruel deceptions as is that of purporting to contact deceased loved ones in return for substantial monetary reward. No basic need of the human condition attracts so many charlatans and frauds as does that particular desire to retain a permanent relationship with a loved one. Yet, to maintain that all mediums are fraudulent in their practice would be to employ the same perverse illogic that maintains that all tellers abscond with bank funds, all policemen accept bribes, all medical doctors are quacks, and all lawyers are ambulance-chasers. From pulpit to peddler, each walk of life has a few bad apples in its barrel. I have interviewed and sat with mediums who were sincere, conscientious, completely frank and honest, and who produced information and knowledge which could not have been gained by any but paranormal means.

Most mediums feel that they can get along without parapsychologists very well. The successful medium does not need to prove anything to his followers—they already believe in his abilities. The tests of the "psi" researcher are tedious and set up to be administered by objective and unemotional personnel. The laboratory certainly does not offer the mood and atmosphere to be found in the seance parlor, and the bright lights are not as conducive to the trance state as is the dimly lighted room. Such laboratory controls are, of course, necessary to unmask the charlatan, but, because mediumistic powers cannot always be turned on and off like an electric light some otherwise sincere mediums have been caught in crude attempts at trickery, because they felt such a desperate need to "prove" their powers.

Eusapia Palladino was one of those who would resort to clumsy tricks in an effort to please the investigators when her otherwise astonishing powers would fail to respond to her will. Hereward Carrington, one of the investigators who examined her, wrote later that when Palladino produced a good seance without any chicanery (and the researchers quickly detected her every time that she did try to employ trickery) the phenomena were 100 per cent genuine. Forty years later, Carrington once again wrote that his personal conviction remained unshaken. ". . . in Eusapia Palladino's seances, genuine physical phenomena of an extraordinary character occurred which (if duly appreciated) would throw an entirely new light upon biology, psychology, and the whole structure of mechanistic science."

After a lifetime devoted to "psi" research, with a special emphasis on the phenomena of mediumship, Carrington concluded that "98 per cent of all such phenomena are fraudulent." But we share Carrington's excitement, when confronted by mediums such as Palladino, that we are left with an uncharted Unknown, as indicated by that researcher-resistant two per cent!

Carrington began a series of tests with another remarkable medium, Eileen J. Garrett, who went on to become a true "medium's-medium." Willing to subject herself to scientific investigation early in her career, Mrs. Garrett was tested by leading universities and scientific groups on both sides of the Atlantic. Mrs. Garrett has always been "on the fence" with regard to the phenomena she produces. This generous woman has literally offered herself to science in a sincere effort to learn more about her "spirits" and to determine whether or not they are what they claim to be. A persistent and highly qualified researcher in her own right, Mrs. Garrett is President of the Parapsychology Foundation, Inc., in New York City and editor of *Tomorrow,* a journal of "psi" research.

Mrs. Garrett is a trance medium, which means that her control, "Uvani," cannot speak through her lips until she has passed into unconsciousness. "Uvani" claims to be a native of Asia Minor who lived about one hundred years ago. All mediums have their spirit guides or controls, most of whom claim to be American Indians or other primitive people. When I once asked a medium why so many mediums were controlled by a "Shooting Star" or a "Redwing," I was told that the Indians maintained an essential relationship with natural forces and an undogmatic approach to the Creator, which is lacking in spirits who arrive from a more civilized era and locale.

Is this spirit guide an entity from the "other side," or is he a level of the medium's transcendent self acting the role?

On the evening of July 8, 1913, "Patience Worth," who claimed to be the spirit of a seventeenth century Englishwoman, became a "control" for Mrs. Pearl Lenore Curran, a young woman in St. Louis, Missouri. Mrs. Curran was not a practicing medium, nor did she have any interest in spiritualism, yet during a period of three years, "Patience Worth" dictated to her a stream of proverbs, lyric poetry, plays, and a number of intricately constructed novels.

Mrs. Curran's formal education had ended with the eighth grade. She seldom read, had never traveled, and was completely unfamiliar with literary people or people of a scholarly bent. At no time in her life had she ever given any indication of a latent creative gift. Yet, of one of the spirit-dictated novels, a reviewer for the *New*

York Times wrote: "Notwithstanding the serious quality and the many pitifulnesses and tragedies of the story it tells, the book has much humor of a quaint, demure kind, a kind of humor that stands out as characteristic of all her work and her personality . . . the plot is contrived with such skill, deftness, and ingenuity as many a novelist in the flesh might well envy."

In an anthology of "best" poetry for the year 1917, "Patience Worth" had five poems selected, as against three of Amy Lowell's, three of Vachel Lindsay's, and one by Edgar Lee Masters.

Was Patience Worth a spirit or a secondary personality of Mrs. Curran's? To her many questioners, investigators, and skeptics, the entity issued a poetic counter-challenge in disgust at their constant harping that she *prove* her existence.

> A phantom? Well enough
> Prove thee thyself to be.
> I say, behold, here I be—
> Buskins, kirtle, cap, and pettyskirts,
> And much tongue.
> Weel, what hast thou to prove thee?

Her point is fairly enough taken. What proof of survival will we accept?

If an honest medium were to tell us that he has contacted the spirit of a close friend or relative who has passed away, what evidence would satisfy us that the "spirit" was indeed who he claimed to be? If a discarnate voice reaches us via a long-distance telephone line, we accept the information that it is our friend calling from Alaska, because we know that he is alive and well. If, however, the same voice were to issue from the mouth of an entranced medium three years after our Alaskan friend had died, how would we determine whether or not the voice was truly that of the departed personality?

I think that we should decide to be quite cunning and

ask the spirit voice questions to which only our friend would know the answer. Intimate, highly personal questions, which would require a memory shared to be properly answered. Perhaps we would deliberately give an incorrect date or name to see if our spirit would notice the error and correct us. We should certainly be on the guard for peculiar mannerisms and idiosyncrasies of thought and speech which were representative of our friend's personality. We should also test the spirit's reactions to ideas and issues about which we knew our friend had strong opinions.

If the spirit passes all of our subtly devised tests with a score of 100 per cent, do we accept this as proof of our friend's survival after death? And what if, as a bonus, the spirit has told us where he hid a certain packet of letters when he was still alive, which, upon our investigation, we find to have been correct information. Do we still maintain our doubt? Or do we, because of our study of "psi" phenomena, rather believe that some telepathic level of the medium's subconscious has penetrated a certain level of our own mind to gain past information about our friend, and that his clairvoyant powers have given us the information about the letters. As we have already observed, it is a great paradox of "psi" research that our ever-increasing knowledge of the limitlessness of Mind has made conclusive proof of survival all the more difficult to secure.

Medium Eileen Garrett, who has said that she is not one "who assumes that the gift of mediumship necessarily brings with it greater insight into the phenomena of that mediumship," authored "The Ethic of Mediumship" for the Autumn, 1960, issue of *Tomorrow*. Mrs. Garrett advises that the medium "will do well to withdraw herself from the ideas thrown out by the inquirer; she must regard herself as a mechanism, clear and simple, through which ideas flow." According to this accomplished medium, those with the gift of mediumship should put themselves into a "receptive mood" which will enable them to "accept the flow of events and ideas to be perceived and known."

"If the medium allows herself to be thus used, things will happen of themselves—a technique old as wisdom itself, and not contradictory to Zen. One allows the feminine or perceptive principle of the unconscious to emerge and thus one is not swamped by the demanding consciousness of the self or the inquirer. This instructive feminine element is, according to Jung, the common property of all mankind. It cannot be coerced, it must be respected and nurtured."

To Mrs. Garrett, mediumship is not a "breaking-down of the personality, but a state of wholeness." She regards the tendency of "enthusiastic sitters to regard the medium as priest or priestess" as the "major danger area in mediumistic activities."

Mrs. Garrett wisely concludes that ". . . Communication with the 'other world' may well become a substitute for living in this world. Understanding that this world, in which we live, has priority in this existence, is at the core of mediumship ethics."

Hereward Carrington concluded, as a result of extensive analysis of mediumship techniques, that an intelligently influenced mechanism was somehow involved in producing the physical phenomena of the seance room.

In an essay written in 1946, Carrington said: "What seemingly happens is that a form of unknown energy . . . issues from the body of the medium, capable of affecting and molding matter in its immediate environment. At times this is invisible; at other times it takes forms and becomes more or less solid, when we have instances of the formation of so-called ectoplasm. It is this semi-material substance which moves matter and even shapes it into different forms."

According to Carrington's observations, this "ectoplasm" issues from various parts of the medium's body—from the fingertips, the solar plexus, and the sexual organs. "It represents a psychic force," wrote Carrington, "as yet unknown to science, but now being studied by scientific men as part and parcel of supernormal biology."

Carrington was certain that this energy had a biological basis and was dependent upon the physical body of the medium for its production—regardless of whether it was directed by the subconscious mind of the medium himself or by the mind of a discarnate personality.

The case of Laura Edmunds seems difficult to account for by offering either a theory of a suddenly developed secondary personality or any kind of conscious or unconscious mental activity. When Miss Edmunds began to speak Greek, it truly seemed as though she had been momentarily possessed by a disembodied entity.

The daughter of a judge of the New York Supreme Court, Laura Edmunds was a quiet, polite girl, who shyly served tea to the guests who dropped by the family home on Sunday afternoons.

On the Sunday that Mr. Evangedides brought a letter of introduction to Judge Edmunds, Laura became suddenly distraught. When she was introduced to the Greek, who had never met any member of the family before, she grabbed his arm and began to talk to him in his native tongue.

Mr. Evangedides turned ash white with shock, and his cup dropped from trembling fingers to shatter on the floor. Tears stung his eyes as he stared at the entranced girl in disbelief.

"She says my son is dead!" the Greek shouted. "In the voice of Botzaris, my dear friend who is dead, she tells me that my son has died!"

The man begged forgiveness and left the Edmunds home at once. Laura shook her head slowly and blinked her eyes as if awakening from a deep sleep. She had no knowledge of what she had said to Mr. Evangedides. With only a "finishing school" education, the girl had no acquaintance with any language other than her own. The next day, Mr. Evangedides notified Judge Edmunds that the terrible news had been confirmed. He was sailing home for Greece at once.

While recovering from a serious illness, Violet Parent, a simple, untutored woman, the wife of a California grocery clerk, had visions of the early mission fathers and their Indian converts. According to Mrs. Parent, the spirits told her where they had buried several crosses and caches of money. Her husband recorded the locations his wife babbled out in her delirium, and later, when she had recovered, the couple and a number of their neighbors went to the spiritually proclaimed spots and dug up several crosses.

Shortly after Mrs. Parent's death, the author, Hamlin Garland, learned of the incident. Together with Mr. Parent and a medium, Mrs. Sophia Williams, Garland unearthed an additional thousand crosses. These artifacts were located in fifty widely separated spots scattered over an area over 600 miles long by 300 miles wide. The spirits' directions were always accurate and to dig was to uncover another of the buried crosses. Each of the designated spots was in a remote, overgrown area where the soil had been undisturbed for years.

Did Mrs. Parent and, later, Mrs. Williams truly receive information concerning the crosses from the spirits of long-dead mission fathers and their Indian converts? Or, again, was it some clairvoyant faculty of mind at work? Certainly trickery seems to be completely ruled out. It is most difficult to conceive of the semi-invalid Mrs. Parent saving up enough money from her husband's meager paycheck to purchase over one thousand antique crosses, then traveling over several hundred miles of rough terrain to dig more than a thousand holes in fifty different areas so that she might claim that "spirits" had told her a secret.

What is the verdict of "psi" researchers concerning the proofs for survival of personality? For the present, the question of survival evidence must be answered by the individual's own interpretation of the knowledge that has been accumulated.

Dr. J. B. Rhine has epitomized the current thinking on survival evidence in these words: "The outcome of the scientific investigation of mediumship is best described as a draw. Hardly anyone would claim that all the investigations of seventy-five years or more have had the effect of disproving the claim that if a man shall die he shall in some manner or other be capable of 'living again.' On the other hand, no serious scientific student of the field of investigation could say that a clear, defensible, scientific confirmation of the hypothesis has been reached."

11.

"PSI" AND PSYCHEDELICS, THE
MIND-EXPANDING DRUGS

Throughout man's tenure on earth, he has often been less than judicious in consuming items of questionable food value. Certain mushrooms, chemically saturated sugarcubes, extracts from cacti, various roots and herbs, and other unlikely substances have been chewed, swallowed, and ingested, not for the purpose of sustaining life, but for the physiological and psychological effects which they have on the body and the brain. Cults of mystical expression have grown up around the use of these substances, and their high-priests continue to proselytize among an insecure and searching citizenry.

"By 1970," Dr. Timothy Leary, primary prophet of the LSD cult, declared recently, "between 10 and 30 million persons, most of them young, will have embarked on voyages of discovery through the limitless inner space of their own minds." According to Leary, these voyagers will return "wiser and more loving" than when they started out. "The next four years, I predict, will be years of mutational conflict. Unless we're very wise and very good to each other there will be many victims."

On May 2, 1938, Dr. Albert Hoffman of the Sandoz Research Laboratories in Basle, Switzerland, first synthesized Lyserg-Saeure-Diaethylamid. Five years later, Dr. Hoffman accidentally inhaled a minute quantity of the drug, while working with other ergot derivatives, and experienced a "not unpleasant inebriation," which consisted of hallucinations that lasted for several hours. Since that time, scientists have been trying to fit LSD-25 and other drugs with hallucinogenic properties into biochemical schemes of many kinds. Substances and chemicals that formerly had an aura of mystery around them, are slowly being broken down by chemical analysis and are now either being hailed as "mind-expanders" or exploited for fast and far-out thrills.

Since the trance state has interested "psi" researchers for many years, much of the recent experimentation with drugs has been followed by parapsychologists with more than a passing concern. Because of the close association of drug-induced hallucinations with mystical visions and trance experiences, it is hoped that a drug will be found that will induce or supplement psychic powers. Although only the barest groundwork has been done, there is some indication that we already possess knowledge of such drugs.

In 1953, Mr. R. Gordon Wasson, a vice-president of the J. P. Morgan Company, and his wife observed a rite of the Mixtec Indians that involved the use of a sacred mushroom. The *curandero,* or witch doctor, was said to have powers of prophecy after he had consumed the mushrooms, and the Wassons were interested in testing his claim.

It was an all-night affair for which the *curandero* had made extensive preparations long before the culmination of the rite began. For five days before and five after, he did not allow himself the company of a woman. He explained his actions to the Wassons by saying he feared he would go mad if he consorted with any female. He drank no alcohol for the same period and fasted for twenty-four hours before the ceremony began. The Wassons first became involved in the ritual at nine o'clock in the evening when the witch doctor called them to a small room containing articles of ceremonial religious observance.

The *curandero* asked the Wassons what information they sought, and the Wassons answered that they wanted to know about their son, Peter, whom they had left in Boston. Then in the small, dark room, illuminated only by candles, the witch doctor began the ceremony. By 10:30, he had eaten fourteen pairs of the mushrooms. Other facets of the rite included the precise arrangement of the ceremonial articles in the room and the rubbing of green tobacco on the *curandero's* head, neck, and stomach. Then the candles were extinguished and they waited.

At 1:00 A.M. the witch doctor claimed that he was receiving a vision of the Wassons' son. He shocked them by saying that Peter needed them because of some emotional crisis in his life. The *curandero* continued, telling them that their son was no longer in the city they had thought he was in and that he was either going to war or joining the army. He ended his string of predictions by stating that a close relative of Mr. Wasson's would become seriously ill within a year.

It was not long after this ceremony that reality bore out the witch doctor's predictions. Peter Wasson had joined the army at the unhappy end of a romance that had left him emotionally distraught. He was only eighteen at the time, but he had joined the service and was shipped to Japan before the Wassons could protest. At the time of the ceremony, he had been not in Boston but in New York. The last portion of the *curandero's* prognostication also came true when one of Mr. Wasson's first cousins died of a heart attack within the one-year period the man had foreseen.

Intrigued by the *curandero's* performance, the Wassons became interested in trying the mushrooms themselves. They pursued the back trails of Mexican bush country until they found a village where the natives were willing to let them join a mushroom ceremony. They were given explicit instructions on what and what not to eat before they consumed the mushrooms. The gathering was held in the basement of one of the Indian dwellings, and each person present consumed six pairs of the greasy-tasting mushrooms within a half an hour. The scene was lit by the moon which shone through an opening in the wall.

About a half an hour later, Wasson said that he felt as if his soul had been scooped from his body and had been projected to a point far away. He went on to describe scenes resembling those commonly described by the users of mind-expansion drugs. Yet, in his case, there was no instance of any kind of prophecy or clairvoyance.

The question remains poised before "psi" researchers without an answer. Can psychedelic ("mind-manifesting") drugs induce or enhance psychic phenomena? There have been very few reports such as the one given by the Wassons, and although the drug-induced experiences are very similar qualitatively to those described by mystics and mediums all over the world, they may be only an accompanying manifestation of the brain state of these sensitives.

While researchers look on, hoping for a break-through, the drug controversy rages. Pointing to the unpredictable results of uncontrolled use of such drugs as LSD-25, mescaline, and psilocybine, critics of unrestricted use of the drugs demand legislation that will curb the distribution of psychedelics. Many recent magazine articles and books stress the detrimental effects some drug users have suffered. Although mind-expansion drugs are not narcotic in the sense that they set up a physical craving within the user, possible long-term effects of the drugs have not yet been determined. If the drug is used as a means of escape from reality, it is possible that a user could become dependent upon it in the same manner that many people become dependent upon alcohol.

Meanwhile, users of the drug have organizations of their own and are determined to meet this challenge to their freedom. They claim that the benefits gained from the psychedelic experience is valuable and should not be forbidden anyone who, of his own volition, would like to try it.

Even though most observers agree that some control is necessary, serious parapsychologists are alarmed that such controversy may yield over-protective legislation, which would hamper the controlled testing of psychedelic potential in the area of "psi" research. Given time, such drugs could help unlock the secrets of telepathy and clairvoyance, and there is much still to be accomplished that could be hampered if legal screws are tightened too far.

Even before medieval witches' potions and the wizards' weird concoctions, men knew about, and used, many varieties of what are now called psychedelics. The ancient Greeks held the mushroom sacred, and some researchers have postulated that the famed Delphic oracle may have been prompted by some form of psychedelic drug, along with the sulfur fumes the entranced woman was supposed to have inhaled. Other cultures have also held the mushroom or the cactus sacred. The Mayan Indians of Central America erected stone monuments to the mushroom earlier than 1000 B.C. These monuments have been found in the tombs of the wealthier citizens of the Mayan culture and for many years were thought to be fertility symbols.

While modern research techniques have shed some light on the nature of the experiences induced by psychedelics, some investigators have begun their research from historical formulas found in ancient manuscripts or inscriptions. Dr. Erick-Will Peuckert, professor at Germany's Gottingen University, is one of these men. Dr. Peuckert has devoted his life to the investigation of ancient formulas, which were purportedly used by followers of the occult in earlier times.

A highly trained man, Dr. Peuckert studies and translates ancient manuscripts, which give step by step prescriptions for the production of what were once considered magic potions. Once these creams and ointments have been manufactured and tested, they can then be analyzed for the chemical components they contain.

Following a formula that claimed to provide the power of attraction between individual members of the opposite sex, Dr. Peuckert combined bodily extracts into a solution which he injected into candies and fruit to be given to test subjects. The young women volunteers responded by being able to pick out the man from whom the solution had been prepared, even if the subjects were in a group of other men who had not participated in the test. Furthermore, the women felt an otherwise unexplainable desire to meet the person with whom they had become chemically enamored.

These experiments, which were performed with tight controls, gave Dr. Peuckert a great deal of sensational publicity in the European press. Not seeking such notoriety, Dr. Peuckert became so upset by the news stories that he has since become very reticent about divulging data about his experiments.

Information about one of his later experiments did find its way into print, however. In an ancient book on witchcraft, Peuckert found a formula for witches' salve which was known to contain such psychedelic drugs as the thorn apple, the Deadly Nightshade, and other regional fruits and roots. Dr. Peuckert and an unnamed attorney friend of his then tested the salve in the ritual manner prescribed by the book of magic.

After the salve had been applied, both men fell into a trance state that resembled sleep. They were both entranced for twenty hours and awakened with mammoth hangovers, complete with cotton mouths, sore throats, and headaches. Dr. Peuckert and his friend both claimed that they had witnessed the wildest orgy known to man— the Black Sabbat of the witches.

The scenes that Dr. Peuckert witnessed seem closely akin to those produced by other psychedelic drugs, except for the heavy emphasis on sexual perversion. Dr. Peuckert's research into the medieval rites may have planted in his mind the suggestion of such scenes which became full-blown hallucinations under the influence of the salve. This is a plausible explanation since psychedelic drugs are used similarly in psychiatry, and it is known that the experiences a subject would like to have before using the drug, affect the experiences which he does have. Thus it is a good explanation—except for the fact that Dr. Peuckert's attorney friend had precisely the same experiences the scientist himself had.

In spite of the hangover both men had upon awakening from the trance, they immediately set about writing separate accounts of what they had envisioned. Except for differences in wording, they described the same scenes. Peuckert's theory is that the Sabbat was often manifest with the use of such salves, and although the people involved actually had no physical experiences, they could be made to confess to their witchcraft because they did not separate hallucinations from reality.

Even though relatively few psychedelically stimulated psychic experiences have been reported, parapsychologists still are optimistic about the value of psychedelics to the work they are doing. Several conferences have been held bringing together experts in pharmacology and parapsychology so that the exchange of information, case studies, and techniques might be facilitated.

Dr. Cedric W. M. Wilson of Bethesda, Maryland, pointed out an important assumption that is being made automatically by those who use psychedelics in their research, i.e. "psi" phenomena are physiological in character. Furthermore, it is assumed that such phenomena are like all other physiological phenomena and are capable of being affected by an external agent.

It is hoped that the proper use of psychedelics will allow "psi" researchers to take some giant steps forward. There have been many complaints that the presently used statistical methods are too slow. One researcher likened the process to measuring the distance to the moon with a yardstick.

Whatever comes of the research, the only certainty is that there is much testing and evaluating left to do. It may be unfortunate that modern science is enslaved to numbers, but the fact is inescapable. Statistical evaluation is now the only known way to adapt a number scheme to "psi" phenomena, and those preoccupied with this approach may be progressing down a blind alley. Dr. Abram Hoffer of Saskatoon, Saskatchewan, Canada, has called for a change in approach. In a symposium on "Methodology of Research" at the conference on Parapsychology and Psychedelics in November of 1958, he stated bluntly that "statistical methods are incorrect" when used to evaluate "psi" phenomena. Dr. Hoffer would like to see an adaptation of "the methods of the biologists and chemists who have made much progress without being over-dependent on statistical methods."

Dr. Hoffer went on to suggest several steps which could give parapsychology a much needed boost. "(1) Study the incidence and prevalence of parapsychological phenomena; (2) Locate people who clearly are gifted; (3) Study environmental conditions which enhance the ability to perceive parapsychologically which will include the setting, the type of phenomena, etc.; (4) Demand a higher order of success, rather than accept successes which are mathematically significant, using statistical theory, but practically insignificant; (5) determine whether the psychedelics will enhance the proven ability of people to sense parapsychological phenomena."

Dr. Roberto Cavanna, an Italian neurochemist, told doctors at Delaware State Hospital of his efforts to give the study of ESP some scientific validity by inducing "psi" phenomena with LSD and psilocybin in a laboratory atmosphere.

Dr. Cavanna feels that there is already enough scientific evidence that verifies the existence of telepathy and has concentrated on the development or encouragement of clairvoyance and precognition in his experiments. "I started with the assumption that ESP does exist," said Dr. Cavanna, "and I began to work with the goal of fitting such phenomena into the framework of scientific understanding."

The neurochemist feels that his work with drugs and "psi" is extremely promising. In one experiment the doctor and his staff give subjects the drugs and hand them a batch of sealed envelopes containing pictures impossible to see with normal perception. The subjects are then asked to describe the pictures contained in the opaque envelopes. Some "extremely sensitive" subjects have been accomplishing remarkable results while under the drugs, according to Dr. Cavanna.

Dr. Sidney Cohen, a Los Angeles psychiatrist-pharmacologist, author of *The Beyond Within,* has written: "It is hardly necessary to invoke supernatural explanations for the mind's more exceptional activities . . . Intuition, creativity, telepathic experiences, prophecy—all can be understood as superior activities of brain-mind function. . . . The experience called hallucinogenic will play a role in leading us into the future. It points out the existence of unique mental states which must be studied and understood."

Dr. Humphrey Osmond, of the New Jersey Neuropsychiatric Institute at Princeton, has been experimenting with hallucinogenics since 1951. It was, in fact, he who coined the world "psychedelic" to describe the effects of the drugs. "We have changed the world so much," he said recently, "that unless we make interior changes we'll soon be in serious trouble."

Dr. Timothy Leary and Dr. Richard Alpert were discharged from their positions at Harvard University in 1963 for their attempts at making "interior changes." Their enthusiasm for the mind-expanding properties of LSD undampened, the two went on to establish a number of colonies of their "International Federation of Internal

Freedom." Leary was arrested in March of 1966 for bringing marijuana into the United States from Mexico. He is, at this writing, awaiting a term in prison.

Law enforcement officials, such as Aaron Koota, Kings County (Brooklyn) district attorney, tend to look upon traffic in LSD and other hallucinogens as just another racket and fear that they will soon have to contend with a black market in the drugs and that it will be aided and abetted by the crime syndicates.

Physicians and psychiatrists warn against the indiscriminate use of LSD.

Dr. Roy Grinker, of Michael Reese Hospital, Chicago, Illinois, editor of the American Medical Association's *Archives of General Psychiatry,* issued a warning that ". . . greater morbidity, and even mortality, is in store for patients unless controls are developed against the unwise use of LSD-25."

Dr. Charles C. Dahlberg of New York is an advocate of the therapeutic uses of LSD, but strenuously warns that it be administered with great care and only to patients who have been studied for six months "to confirm the absence of a hidden psychotic process."

Dr. D. C. McClelland of Harvard University stated in a staff memorandum: "It is probably no accident that the society which most consistently encourages the use of these substances, India, produced one of the sickest social orders ever created by mankind, in which thinking men spend their time lost in the Buddha position under the influence of drugs exploring consciousness, while poverty, disease, social discrimination, and superstition reached their highest and most organized form in all history."

What does LSD do and how does it act?

One team of investigators grouped the following primary effects: 1.) a feeling of being one with the universe; 2.) recognition of two identities; 3.) a change in the usual concept of self; 4.) new perceptions of space and time; 5.) heightened sensory perceptions; 6.) a feeling that one has been touched by a profound understanding of religion or philosophy; 7.) a gamut of rapidly changing emotions; 8.) increased sensitivity for the feelings of others; 9.) such psychotic changes as illusions, hallucinations, paranoid delusions, severe anxiety.

Dr. Leszek Ochota, a member of the investigational drug branch of the Food and Drug Administration, distinguished four stages of LSD action in the May 14, 1966, issue of *The New Republic*.

1. Initial, lasting for ½ to ¾ hours after oral ingestion of 100 to 150 micrograms of LSD, and producing slight nausea, some anxiety, dilation of pupils, tachycardia, etc.;

2. "Experience," lasting for 1 to 4 to 8 hours, and consisting of illusions, hallucinations, associated with significant alteration of orientation (mainly impaired for time, rarely for place), of consciousness (confusional states, dreamlike revivals of past traumatic events or childhood memories), of sensory perception (in addition to visual illusions, hallucinations and synesthesias—distortion of space and perspective), or motor coordination (impaired on testing), of mood affectivity (anxiety, euphoria, hypomania, ecstasy, autistic withdrawal), of ideation (flight of ideas, ideas of reference, impairment of concentration and intelligence on testing), and alteration of personality (dissolution of personality by depersonalization and derealization, impairment of conscience and of acquired social and cultural customs);

3. Recovery, lasting for several hours and consisting of "waves of normality alternating with waves of abnormality";

4. Aftermath, consisting of fatigue and tension during the following day.

LSD is not addictive. It is, in fact, self-limiting. If one

were to take the drug for three days in a row, it would no longer produce a psychic effect. A week or longer would have to pass before the drug would again "expand the mind."

Why, then, should LSD and the other psychedelics be treated as if they were poisons by law enforcement agencies and by certain physicians and psychiatrists? The simple fact is that not enough is yet known about psychedelics to recommend prescribing the drugs and popping them into everyone's mouth in the hope that each of us is capable of creating his own inner "brave new worlds."

For one thing, LSD can cause permanent psychotic reactions and psychic splits that may never heal. Add this fact along with the estimate that approximately five per cent of the world's population is predisposed to schizophrenia and you arrive at one very strong argument for supervised usage of the drug. Even Dr. Timothy Leary has swallowed a few rash statements and announced that "not everyone has an absolute right to do what he wants with his own head."

For another, we as yet have no idea how LSD affects the brain and the body. Some researchers have suggested that since the substance itself leaves the system so rapidly it must trigger the discharge of some as yet unidentified bodily substance. At least one investigator has noticed a change in the aging process among native shamans and diviners who steadily partake of their own home-brewed psychedelics. Rapid aging might be an as yet unforeseen result of extensive use of psychedelics.

Then, too, some psychiatrists maintain that a psychotic disturbance can occur days, weeks, even months after receiving LSD. Others hasten to add that this could only happen if the individual were already psychically disturbed, but this argument only emphasizes the need for the careful screening of those who use hallucinogens.

Dr. Ochota lists the "more evident dangers of the prolonged adverse reactions from hallucinogens" as based on FDA research. These are: "mood swings, including depression, which may lead to suicide, and euphoria, which may lead to socially embarrassing situations; time and space distortions, presenting obvious traffic dangers; hallucinations, which are perilous out-of-doors; impulsive behavior, wandering and absent-mindedness, all of which may endanger the user and those with him."

And so the controversy over the use of psychedelics rages on. Parapsychologists can only look on and hope that the increasing legal clamps will not hamper the promising research that has got under way.

12.

ESP IN THE SPACE AGE

Space age travel has put several thorny problems to the men who dream of traveling to the stars. It is unfortunate, but true, that conveying information energy by means of electromagnetic waves is a time-consuming process. A message sent by conventional radio from the sun takes over eight minutes before it arrives at the earth. A future explorer at the fringes of the solar system, sending a message from the frozen crust of Pluto, for example, will have to wait at least eight hours for a reply by conventional means. Once man gets out of the solar system and to the nearest stars the time lag will be measured not in minutes or hours, but in years.

Some scientists hope that "psi" research may come up with the answer that will eliminate the time lag problem in space age communication. A team of scientists from the Westinghouse Electric Corporation began the study of ESP as a possible vehicle of communication as part of the company's astronautics institute. Soviet Russia has been trying to probe the nature of telepathy since the second decade of this century.

There are many examples of long-range telepathic communication. In 1937 a Russian flyer, Sigismund Levanevsky, set out on what was then a daring flight over the polar regions of the earth. The flyer and his five crew members vanished without so much as a whimper of their shortwave, and the Soviet government prevailed upon a well-known British Arctic explorer, Sir Hubert Wilkens, to conduct a search for the missing airmen. Just before the explorer was to leave on his search,

October 15, 1937, he had lunch with Harold Sherman, a psychical researcher and author, and the two men agreed to attempt to remain in contact with each other by telepathy during the days of the search. They agreed to a time when they both would concentrate on telepathic rapport—11:30 to midnight on Monday, Tuesday and Thursday evenings—and also on the type of information which they would try to convey. Sir Hubert would try to "transmit" specific information concerning the position and progress of the expedition.

On the first, and all succeeding sessions, Sherman retired to his study and darkened all the lights before sitting in his chair facing a blank wall. He kept a pad and pencil at his side and a flashlight, but that was all. As he began concentrating, he almost immediately began receiving a series of vivid yet very confused images of what appeared to be the Arctic. He described them as "a maze of kaleidoscope scenes." Not quite sure what to make of the images, Sherman realized that such transmission, if indeed it were transmission, was of no use since no intelligible information was transmitted. His desire was to get a clear picture of what the explorer was in the process of doing. He let this idea flow through the conscious portion of his mind, and by the force of his will, the maze of images congealed into one. At that time, Wilkens was over a thousand miles away, but the images were very vivid. Sherman was disappointed, however, when a few days later he received a letter from Sir Hubert stating that the man had found it impossible to spend the time allotted for the attempt at telepathic communication. The demands of his search mission took up every waking moment of his time.

Nonetheless, Sherman wrote the impressions that he thought he had received from the explorer in a letter and sent them to one of his bases in the Arctic. Both men were surprised to find that the images which Sherman received had indeed been of things that Wilkens had observed. The transmission had occurred even without any conscious effort on Wilkens' part. The men continued to work in the same fashion: Sherman collecting images and then transmitting them by mail to the Arctic bases, Wilkens mailing Sherman the corroborating accounts.

The information was never as precise as a formal report would have been, but it was surprisingly accurate. Sherman was able to determine the location of the expedition, the events which the explorer observed, and the mechanical difficulties Sir Hubert was having with the plane that he flew.

Reginald Iversen, who had been hired by the *New York Times* to keep in radio contact with the search expedition, found that the sunspot and magnetic conditions made regular communication impossible, and he was able to get through to the search party on only a relatively few occasions. In an affidavit, which the radioman signed after the unsuccessful search for the Russian flyers had been completed, Iversen testified that Sherman had received more accurate knowledge via telepathy than he had been able to gain from his sporadic radio contact with Wilkens.

Thus there is reason to expect that information can be transferred with the use of telepathy. But even if such transmission can be established, there are still many questions which must be answered before its value for interstellar communications can be determined. For example, the exact nature of the energy involved is yet to be identified. If telepathy is electromagnetic in character, then it would be impossible for it to travel faster than the speed of light, and it would not be of any advantage over conventional communication. If it is not, its speed will have to be determined. It is possible that facts uncovered in research on telepathy will require an entirely new concept of time.

Although telepathy is one of the most promising branches of "psi" research with "scientific potential," it is not by any means the only area which may have space age applications. The advantages of being able to control clairvoyant powers have already been made obvious to police departments all over the world. There are many famous cases where a clairvoyant has been able to locate a missing body or identify a criminal without being near the scene of the crime, or even the city where it was committed. In some cases, mechanical difficulties within machines have been located by bringing a clairvoyant's attention to the case, as in the case of Croiset and Captain Jansen's ship engine.

In less spectacular fields, where man is trying to divine reasons for human behavior, "psi" research may perfect useful new tools for exploring the human psyche. Very little is known about the thought process itself, but if a psychiatrist were able to mentally probe his patient's mind, he might be in a much better position to treat him. Although such speculation is interesting, researchers have had several disappointments in trying to determine the nature of schizophrenia with the use of psychedelics. It was assumed that the experiences of people under the influence of a drug called mescaline were similar to the experiences of schizophrenics. It was then hypothesized that a normal person experiencing the effects of the drug could then report to psychologists the nature of his experience, giving them a new insight into the mental disease. Superficially, these two kinds of experience seemed to be alike, but the actual insight gained by the researchers was of no particular value to the psychological study of schizophrenia. The thought process is more complicated than it appears on the surface.

In the borderline between psychology and parapsychology is the use of trance states for investigation of both normal and paranormal phenomena. Hypnotic and drug-induced trance states seem to be easy avenues of entry into the inner recesses of man's mind. Hypnosis has been a psychiatric tool for many years, even though its use has gone in and out of vogue several times. "Psi" research with hypnosis and psychedelics may unlock secrets of the trance states, which will allow man to understand himself more thoroughly in the world of the future.

As with any other natural ability the application of psychic powers is at the discretion of man. During the Korean war, the public became acquainted with the term "brain-washing." This domination of men's minds has become one of the most useful weapons in the propagandists' arsenal. With the use of what most experts term a kind of post-hypnotic suggestion, propagandists have been able to extract confessions of crimes never committed, to reverse lifelong loyalties, and to blur any conventional notion of the difference between truth and falsehood.

In a famous case, Dr. John D. Hayes, a Presbyterian minister and teacher, who had lived in China his entire life, was accused, along with a fellow missionary, of being an American spy. A grueling trial, which was held at Kweiyang, lasted for seventy-five days. During this time, Dr. Hayes was kept on what later looked like a rigorously planned program to keep him in a kind of mental never-never land. This state was projected by the use of two pivots—a constant barrage of accusations during the day, and the evocation of nostalgic dreams of home during the night. At the end of this psychological program, Dr. Hayes awoke one morning to find two memory-patterns in his mind. These memories, if true, showed clearly that the two missionaries had conspired against the People's Republic of China. In one, Dr. Hayes' friend asked if he should get rid of "the radio," and in the other, this same friend told Dr. Hayes that he had got rid of "the radio." Although the Chinese were successful in planting these "memories" in Dr. Hayes, they were not successful with his friend. When Dr. Hayes confessed, his friend denied that he had any knowledge of such a conspiracy. The trial ended with both of the men being deported because of the uncorroborating testimony.

One phase of Soviet experiments with telepathy has centered around the induction of hypnosis at long range. Some of these experiments have been successful at distances of over a thousand miles!

It is well known that certain drugs induce states of mind that make individuals more susceptible to advertising. Research with psychedelics show that certain areas of the brain, including centers of pleasure and depression, can be chemically stimulated. Other sections of the brain can be stimulated electronically. If some combination of psychedelic stimulus and a "psi" phenomenon such as telepathically induced hypnosis could be welded together, a psychic weapon of terrifying significance would emerge.

Although such research is in infant stages, many sources all over the world indicate that the terrifying possibilities do exist. The application of "psi" research is in the hands of man. It may allow him instantaneous communication across the reaches of space, or it might allow a few fiendish minds to psychologically dominate the world.

13.

"PSI" RESEARCH BEHIND
THE IRON CURTAIN

The most intensive state-sponsored "psi" research being carried on in the world today is being conducted behind the Iron Curtain. Russia and many of her satellites have coordinated programs for the investigation of ESP centered around telepathy. The goal of this research is to add another useful tool to the collection of implements which the state already has gathered.

Unknown to the rest of the world, and to most of the communist countries, research into the nature and uses of telepathy has been going on in the Soviet Union for more than forty years. One of the early Soviet experimenters was V. M. Bekhterev, the leader in a series of tests in which telepathic communication was attempted between man and animals, specifically, a dog. Bekhterev and his associates obtained for their experiments an animal trainer, V. L. Durov, who had trained a dog named Mars.

The experiments were to test Durov's ability to communicate with the dog without giving an audible or visible signal. In one demonstration, Durov was to command the dog to bark a specified number of times. Bekhterev's assistant took the dog to a room some distance from the other two men. The only stipulation the animal trainer had put on the test was that the number of barks not exceed seven, lest the dog begin barking continually out of habit.

When Bekhterev and Durov were alone in the room, the animal trainer was given a slip of paper which had the specified number of responses the dog was to make at Durov's signal to bark. No word was exchanged. But the number on the slip of paper was fourteen—exactly double the maximum number Durov had specified. The trainer was puzzled, but after writing something on the paper, he continued with the silent experiment.

Bekhterev's assistant, who had taken the dog away from Durov, kept a meticulous watch on its activities. This man had not been informed of the number of barks specified for the test, his only task being to observe and record everything that the dog did. At first Mars did nothing. He lay on the floor. Then the observer saw him draw his body up on his forelegs and cock his ears. He barked seven times before he settled back to the floor. Thinking that the experiment was over, the man wanted to take the dog back to the trainer. But before he could move toward Mars, the dog did exactly the same thing again, drawing himself up on his forelegs, cocking his ears, and barking seven times.

Afraid that Mars would simply start barking and not stop, Durov had divided the command into two parts of seven each. He had written "7 + 7" on the slip which Bekhterev had given him.

Other more complicated experiments were carried out by this team of researchers. In one particularly striking instance, the dog was given an order to find an object he had never seen, within a room he had never entered. In addition, the object (a telephone directory) was placed on one of three tables of varying heights, all of which were out of the normal vision of the dog unless he stood on his hind legs. Many other objects were scattered around the room and on each of the tables.

Durov took the dog's head into his hands and stared intently into his eyes, mentally giving him the command to retrieve the directory. Durov repeated the procedure three times, then Mars ran out of the room and into the one he had never before entered. The dog propped his forelegs up on the first two tables, but not finding what he wanted, went to the third where he picked out the directory from among the other objects and brought it back to the laboratory.

Even though the accuracy of these experiments is astonishing, it did little to stir the interest of the Soviet leaders at the time. The same objection that existed in the West, existed behind the Iron Curtain: this type of experiment is not subject to any kind of number scheme, thus it does not enhance the knowledge of telepathy, except to reconfirm its existence.

In the paper written at the conclusion of these experiments, Bekhterev assumed that telepathy was some form of electromagnetic energy. He reasoned that such energy was somehow modulated and transmitted from Durov to the dog, which received and interpreted the modulated wave. This paper expressed the opinion that the chemical changes in the brain induced electric currents which stimulated the wave transmission and modulation.

Later experiments with Durov and Mars seemed to confirm Bekhterev's opinions. B. B. Kazhinskyi, another Soviet scientist, continued the experiments which Bekhterev had begun. The bulk of his arguments centered around the use of an electromagnetic screening device known as a Faraday cage. The Faraday cage is a chamber which is usually lined with a layer of lead and mercury surrounded by an electromagnetic field which reduces the number of penetrating electromagnetic waves to practically nothing.

When Durov was put in the Faraday cage and attempted to give mental commands to Mars, the dog failed to respond to any of the orders. When the door of the cage was open, however, Mars again responded to his master's mental signals.

Other experimenters also attempted to test the hypothesis that telepathy was a form of electromagnetic signal. L. Vodolazskyi and T. Gursteyn, using a subject who had been hypnotized, shut him up in an electro-magnetically screened chamber. The hypnotist, who was stationed in a separate room, mentally suggested that the subject perform certain tasks. This experiment was carefully planned so that the door to the screening chamber could be opened and closed without the knowledge of either the subject or the hypnotist. As long as the subject was screened electromagnetically from the hypnotist, none of the man's telepathic suggestions were followed. When the door was opened, the subject responded to his suggestions with a high degree of accuracy.

These and other experiments (one of which even attempted to direct the telepathic signals with the use of a metal mirror) seemed to confirm the hypothesis that telepathy was basically electromagnetic in character. This school of Russian parapsychologists was under the influence of the Italian neurophysiologist, F. Cazzamalli. His conclusions also pointed to an electromagnetic wave character for telepathic signals. His experiments have been criticized several times since the 1920's when they were performed, however, since they were not conducted under very rigid controls.

This group, as convincing a front as they presented, did not drown the skepticism about the electromagnetic wave character of telepathic signals. Even while these experiments were being carried out, one of Bekhterev's pupils, L. L. Vasiliev, was disturbing this pat theory with some astounding results of his own.

Vasiliev's original experiments were conducted with the use of subjects and hypnotists. His concern was not to solicit responses from the suggestion of the hypnotists via telepathic means, but to induce the trance state itself by the use of telepathy.

The subject was given an inflated rubber ball which was attached by a hose to a pressure-sensitive recording device. He was then instructed to squeeze the ball with his hand. These contractions were recorded as notches on the moveable graph. When the subject was hypnotized, the rhythmic contractions would stop, and the notches would no longer appear on the graph. The subject and the hypnotist were separated by two intervening walls. The room between housed the recording equipment and those in charge of monitoring it.

Time for each attempt of this telepathic hypnosis was determined by the use of a roulette wheel and was thus completely random. In 1932, Vasiliev was fortunate enough to find three very sensitive subjects with whom the goal of long-distance hypnosis was attainable. When the hypnotist was instructed to induce a trance on the person he could not see, he was able to perform the feat. Later, when instructed to bring the subject out of the trance, the hypnotist was again able to accomplish this by the force of his will, without once coming in contact with the subject during the entire course of the test.

As work in this series of experiments continued, a few unforeseen problems began to develop. After a number of trials, the subjects became so accustomed to the surroundings and the preparations for the tests, that they would fall into trance automatically. Such auto-hypnosis is not uncommon, even when the hypnotist is not trying to induce the trance state via telepathy. But even when this occurred, the effect of a telepathic impulse was striking. A subject could be put in a trance state two or three times faster when the hypnotist attempted to send a telepathic signal than when the auto-hypnosis was allowed to occur. As these tests with the same subject continued, it became more difficult to bring the subject out of the trance state with the use of telepathy. Yet telepathy was still a factor, as the hypnotist could revive the subject momentarily before he would fall back into the trance state.

Because these results were consistently good, Vasiliev was able to devise even more interesting tests. He placed the subjects within chambers that were heavily sealed from all forms of electromagnetic radiation. In this test the subjects responded exactly as they had without the shielding, contradicting the results of the other Soviet experimenters. Vasiliev's rigidly controlled experiments showed that there was more to telepathy than electromagnetic waves. A Russian physicist, V. Arkadev, supported Vasiliev's contention by saying that the intensity of the waves which could be spawned by the electric currents in the brain is so low that dissipation occurs very close to the skull. Even though it has been proven that electromagnetic radiation can affect the central nervous system, the electromagnetic waves generated by the electric currents which are constantly surrounding modern man are of a much higher intensity than any kind of electromagnetic radiation the brain could muster.

These contradictory results have not yet been explained, but Soviet scientists and "psi" researchers outside the Iron Curtain have since leaned away from the theory that telepathic signals are electromagnetic waves. Even more than in other scientific endeavors, psychic researchers must be certain to eliminate all prejudice from their minds. It is very possible that a researcher's brain state may have as much effect on a subject as an intended telepathic signal. The early Soviet experiments may have shown that telepathy was electromagnetic in character, because the investigators, under the heavy influence of the Italian Cazzamalli wanted or expected them to show it. A prejudice—which cannot be separated from the mind—may be a decisive factor in any experiments involving psychic phenomena. These possibilities only add to the difficulty of conducting experiments, but they cannot be ignored.

Vasiliev is now head of the parapsychology department at Leningrad University. Since his experiments in the 1930's, the Soviets have no doubt learned much more about telepathy than they have committed to publication or offered to share with the West.

"Psi" research has posed a curious problem behind the Iron Curtain. The official communist position is that thinking cannot be separated from the brain. Soviet parapsychologists are quick to point out that the transfer of thoughts does not necessarily occur in telepathy, only the transfer of information contained in thoughts. Even though this has been generally accepted, it is still a rather uneasy position.

The touchiest point seems to be concerned with the possibility of life after death. Such a notion is heresy, opposed to communist dogma. Any explanation of psychic phenomena which drifts away from an explanation involving matter and energy in conventional forms is treading dangerously near the spiritual explanation, which is impossible for the communists to accept because their dogma proclaims it false.

The official communist position has been known to change in many other areas, and the apparent potential of such phenomena as telepathy cannot be overlooked. The practical applications of ESP may already have forced Iron Curtain dogma to expand another notch, as certain reports indicate that "psi" research is being carried out at a vigorous pace.

14.

LATEST EXPERIMENTS IN ESP

At the American Society for Psychical Research all-day ESP forum held on November 20, 1965, in New York City, Dr. Gardner Murphy, President of the A.S.P.R., told assembled parapsychologists and representatives from other disciplines that " . . . Progress in parapsychology in the direction of science calls for major, sustained effort . . . devoted to the building of theories and systematic models. The primary need is not for lots and lots of further little experiments, but for bold and sound model building."

Dr. Murphy concluded his address, "Advancement of Parapsychology as a Science," by stating that the future of parapsychology as a science is going to depend on multidisciplinary co-operation between the "psi" researcher and "the medical man, the anthropologist, the sociologist, the physicist, the biologist, the psychologist, and a great many other kinds of people working together within a broad perspective and giving each other mutual support."

Among those engaged in "bold and sound model building" are Montague Ullman, M.D., Stanley Krippner, Ph.D., and Sol Feldstein, B.E.E., who conduct the "Dream Laboratory" at Maimonides Hospital, Brooklyn, New York. This unique laboratory was established in 1962 for the purpose of investigating the possibility of telepathic transfer of information from an agent to a sleeping subject. The men conducting the series of experiments, all members of the Department of Psychiatry at Maimonides, were aware of the literature of psychology, which conjectures about apparent telepathic dreams that occur between patient and analyst during psychotherapy, and the literature of parapsychology, which observes that sleep provides favorable conditions for the occurrence of paranormal phenomena.

In a paper prepared for presentation at the annual convention of the American Psychological Association, New York City, 1966, the experimenters state: "In many such spontaneous cases the telepathic message appeared to be dramatically incorporated into the text of the dream, hence the desirability of developing a methodology for investigating dreams from this point of view."

The use of an electroencephalograph and the use of Rapid Eye Movement (REM) techniques in monitoring dreams enabled the Dream Laboratory to move from "an anecdotal and clinical level of observation to an experimental level." Their working hypothesis stated that the dreams of a sleeping subject would reflect the telepathic influence of an agent, who would be concentrating on target material.

Twelve paid volunteers (seven male, five female) were selected as subjects for the series of experiments. Criteria for the selection of the subjects included the ability to fall asleep easily, to dream frequently, to remember their dreams. Subjects were also selected on the basis of whether or not they had positive attitudes toward the possibility of telepathy.

Target material consisted of twelve prints of famous paintings, chosen on the basis of simplicity and distinctness of detail. Each print was used only once by the agent during the study. In addition to each subject later ranking target material for correspondence to his dream experience, three outside judges independently evaluated the dreams, which had been immediately recorded and transcribed upon the subject's awakening.

Each subject was tested individually on a different evening. He was instructed to report to the Dream Laboratory no later than 11:00 P.M. He was taken to the sleep room, had the electrodes connected, made comfortable, and left to fall asleep. Adjoining the sleep room was the monitoring room in which the experimenter, the EEG, and the recording equipment were located. The agent and the target material were situated in a room at the other end of the building. No conscious or unconscious verbal communication was possible between agent and subject.

In his room, the agent selected a target painting using a procedure based on a random number table. After he had selected the envelope for that night, the remaining envelopes were re-filed before he opened the envelope containing the target. For a period of about 30 minutes, and at various times during the evening, the agent spent time associating with the painting and jotting down his impressions.

The experimenter, who was never told which target was being used by the agent, awakened the subject by means of the intercom after five to ten minutes of REMs indicated that the subject had been dreaming.

"Please tell me your dream or anything that was going through your mind when you were awakened," he would ask the subject. "Is there anything else? Think for a moment. Does anything else occur to you in conjunction with the dream? Does it remind you of anything? Please go back to sleep."

A post-sleep interview was held over the intercom as soon as the subject awakened in the morning. At the completion of the interview, the experimenter entered the sleep room, disconnected the electrodes, and gave the subject an envelope which contained copies of all twelve of the target paintings. The subject was then asked to rank the target which he thought most closely corresponded with his dreams. Copies of the target material were then sent to the three judges along with typed transcripts of the subject's dream reports and his associational material.

I am indebted to Dr. Stanley Krippner for permission to examine some of the anecdotal material connected with subject responses.

The target *Animals* by Tamayo depicts two dogs with exaggerated teeth snarling over scattered bones. There is a large black rock in the background. One subject, a female teacher, saw herself at a banquet ". . . eating something like rib steak. And this friend of mine was there . . . and people were talking about how she wasn't very good to invite for dinner because she was very conscious of other people getting more to eat than she got, especially, meat . . ."

Zapatistas by Orozco portrays a group of Mexican revolutionaries walking against a backdrop of bold mountains and clouds. A male psychologist dreamed of ". . . a storm. Rainstorm. It reminds me of traveling . . . approaching a rainstorm . . . For some reason, I get a feeling of memory, now of New Mexico when I lived there. There are a lot of mountains around New Mexico. Indians, pueblos. Now my thoughts go to almost as though I were thinking of another civilization."

In *The Sacred Fish* by De Chirico, two dead fish lay on a wooden slab which has been placed in front of a candle. A female artist, acting as a subject, dreamed of "death, of going swimming, of a wooden table, and of lighting a candle." She also dreamed of a friend who kept asking her how to spell "fish" in French.

The first series of twelve targets served as a screening procedure for the second group of tests conducted by the Dream Laboratory. In this series of tests, the most gifted subject was selected from the original twelve and paired with the better agent of the two who had been "transmitting" during the first group. Again, the hypothesis was that "telepathic effects in the dreams of a sleeping subject can be experimentally demonstrated."

The results of the second series, according to the judges, was that "the actual targets were ranked significantly more favorably than expected by chance whether that ranking was executed on the basis of the dream material alone or on the dreams in combination with the subject's associations to them."

Boats on the Beach by Van Gogh produced a dream which made the subject think of ". . . something to do with a painter. It makes me think of Van Gogh, perhaps . . . on a boardwalk or a beach . . . The sea coast. The place is slightly elevated. The boards or planks seem to stand out."

Dali's *The Sacrament of the Last Supper* brought some provocative dream associations. The subject saw "a glass of wine, very unusual wine." He saw a group of people among whom ". . . someone was trying to do something that wasn't good—destructive perhaps . . . One of them was not good." The subject also made a number of references to a "magician" or a "small town doctor."

Because the experimenters were so intrigued with the subject's many associations with Christ-figures when Dali's painting was employed as the target, they departed from their normal procedure of random selection and had the agent use the *Sacrament of the Last Supper* on a later night. On this occasion, the subject had six dreams, which included impressions of ". . . a dozen or so men pulling a fishing boat ashore right after having returned from a catch. The fishermen dream makes me think of the Mediterranean area, perhaps even some sort of Biblical time. Right now my associations are of the fish and the loaf, or even the feeding of the multitudes."

In a later dream on that night, the subject saw a Christmas catalog. In yet another, he thought of a picture where ". . . a doctor is sitting beside a child that is ill . . . It's called 'The Physician.' "

When Chagall's *Paris from a Window* was the target, the subject dreamed of " . . . walking in the French Quarter . . . It would definitely be in the early nineteenth century."

Experimenters Ullman, Krippner, and Feldstein feel strongly that their accumulated data suggest that, "as hypothesized, the transfer of information from an agent to a sleeping subject, by means other than the ordinary sensory channels of communication, can be experimentally demonstrated under the conditions described."

Dr. Karlis Osis, of the American Society for Psychical Research, is currently engaged in research with ESP and the effects of distance.

Dr. A. H. Esser, T. L. Etter, and W. B. Chamberlain, Research Facility, Rockland State Hospital, are conducting an inquiry into whether there are any "physiological concomitants to extrasensory communication," and are "pursuing our research with a view toward designing an experiment which satisfies the rigor of repeatability."

According to Dr. J. G. Pratt, University of Virginia, School of Medicine, their research program is "subject-centered; that is to say, the emphasis is placed upon selecting for investigation individuals who show, to a striking degree, one or another of the psi abilities that we want to study."

Dr. Gertrude R. Schmeidler, Department of Psychology, City College of the City University of New York, is currently studying the varying effects of grouping congenial or uncongenial pairs for ESP tests. ". . . the second score will be even worse than the first for subjects who are reserved or hostile, and the second score will be better than the first for subjects predicted to be congenial," Dr. Schmeidler said of her hypothesis in the *Journal* of the American Society for Psychical Research, Volume 60, July, 1966.

The Dream Laboratory at Maimonides Hospital of Brooklyn is presently working with ESP in hypnotically induced dreams. According to Dr. Stanley Krippner, ". . . Perhaps the most important aspect of the study is the inclusion of a control group which receives the same amount of encouragement, persuasion, and suggestion as the experimental group—but without formal trance induction. This type of control has been lacking in most studies and therefore one cannot be sure whether the results would have been similar without hypnotic induction."

Serious researchers have increased their experiments in an all-out effort to meet the challenge offered by orthodox science. Tighter controls, new methods of evaluation, greater awareness of the human element are all being incorporated into current research in ESP.

Dr. Henry Margenau, Higgins Professor of Physics and Natural Philosophy, Yale University, was asked by Dr. Gardner Murphy, President of the A.S.P.R., to give the luncheon address at the ESP forum in New York City. Dr. Margenau chose as his topic, "ESP in the Framework of Modern Science." In this address, the Yale physicist urged parapsychologists to develop theory.

"No amount of empirical evidence, no mere collection of facts, will convince all scientists of the veracity and the significance of your reports. You must provide some sort of model . . . you must advance bold constructs —constructs connected within a texture of rationality—in terms of which ESP can be theoretically understood . . ."

According to Dr. Margenau, the scientific climate for the acceptance of "psi" research has never been better. "To put it bluntly," he said, "science no longer contains absolute truths.

"We have begun to doubt such fundamental propositions as the principle of the conservation of energy, the principle of causality, and many other commitments which were held to be unshakeable and firm in the past. And this has, I think, an interesting bearing upon your own pursuits, for it means that the old distinction between the natural and the supernatural has become spurious. That distinction rested upon a dogmatism, a scientific dogmatism, which supposed that everything in the way of fundamental facts and basic matters was known and that there was an obvious distinction between what was possible and what was not possible. Today we know that there are many phenomena on the fringe, on the periphery of present-day science, which are not yet understood, which are still obscure, but which will nevertheless be encompassed by the scientific method and by scientific understanding in the future."

Dr. Margenau feels that the parapsychologist is not "likely to find theories which will illuminate his area of interest already prepared by physicists." He advises the "psi" researcher to "strike out on his own and probably reason in bolder terms than present-day physics suggests."

The Yale physicist and natural philosopher concluded his address by declaring: "The concepts of parapsychology may well turn out to be at first completely different from the concepts of contemporary physics. The other behavioral sciences are not fashioned precisely after the patterns of inorganic behavior; yet they are acceptable and they succeed . . . Tolerate the strident critical voices of hard-boiled, pragmatic, and satisfied scientists without too much concern, and continue your own painstaking search for an understanding of new kinds of experience, possibly in terms of concepts which now appear strange."

15.

ESP—TEST IT YOURSELF

Who has ESP? We have already answered that question by theorizing that extrasensory perception may be an evolutionary remnant in all of us which has become inhibited by our cultural pattern. Our modern world presents us with a complexly structured existence that depends on the five senses with their more reliable and biologically more useful data for effective functioning. Nature may be suppressing our "psi" abilities in favor of sense perceptions. "Psi" phenomena appear to be products of the unconscious, and the person with high ESP abilities is seldom able to tell the researcher anything at all about how they work or even when they work.

Over the past several years, however, parapsychologists have been able to make some generalizations about certain factors which have been shown to accompany success in ESP.

A belief that ESP exists and that he can control or exercise certain aspects of "psi" phenomena is essential, it seems, for a subject to perform well in any kind of parapsychological testing.

Contrary to a popular notion among laymen, intelligence has little connection to paranormal ability. There is no conclusive evidence to indicate that either high or low intelligence contributes to one's ESP prowess.

Neither is it the "odd" or poorly adjusted members of society who most often demonstrate high "psi" abilities. As a matter of fact quite the contrary is true. Those who are well-adjusted socially and who are possessed of an extraverted rather than an introverted personality are the ones who consistently score higher in ESP tests.

Current research indicates that manifestation of ESP abilities are extremely widespread in the human population, existing in nearly everyone, and evidencing themselves in an occasional dramatic incident in perhaps one-third or more of the population.

In laboratory testing, parapsychologists have noted that the emotional and intellectual attitude of the subject is of great importance. The most outstanding subjects have an intense interest in attaining a good score, a high belief that they can achieve such a score, and a continuing self-confidence in their psychic abilities.

If you are a firm believer in ESP but have never had the opportunity to be tested by a parapsychologist, there are a number of simple tests which, with the aid of a partner, you can perform in your own home. If these tests are performed correctly, they may help you to convince yourself of the existence of your own "psi" abilities.

USING THE ESP (ZENER) CARDS TO TEST FOR TELEPATHY AND CLAIRVOYANCE—The Zener cards, which Dr. J. B. Rhine and his colleagues use at Duke University, are quite easily obtainable. As previously described, the Zener cards consist of five easily recognizable geometric designs.

As a friend is thoroughly shuffling the cards, number a sheet of paper from 1 to 25. After the cards have been shuffled, hand the paper to your friend so that he might keep a record of your choices. Either turn your back to your friend and the cards or leave the room.

At an unspoken sound signal (i.e. a finger snap, the ringing of a bell), proceed to "guess" each card as your friend takes it from the pack. Your "agent" must record both your choice and the correct geometric design beside the corresponding number on the sheet of paper. It is important that you maintain an attitude of complete calm throughout the test. Remember to relax and allow your subconscious to provide the choice. Conscious thinking will only block your ESP processes.

When you have named all twenty-five cards, have your friend total your correct choices and compute your percentage of accurate guesses. Chance or normal probability will be five correct choices out of twenty-five. If you, as the percipient, have named more than five cards correctly, you have performed better than the laws of chance allow.

In testing for telepathy, the agent looks at the card as he gives the signal to make a new choice. To test for clairvoyance, the agent must not look at the card until *after* he has signaled the percipient to make his guess. In either test, the results of the run must be recorded.

If Zener cards are unavailable, an ordinary pack of playing cards can be used with a few simple alterations. Remove the four face cards of each suit and discard the remainder of the deck. You will then have sixteen guesses to make instead of twenty-five, and you will make your choice of suit—Spades, Diamonds, Clubs, Hearts—instead of geometric design. Again, your friend must record your choices on a sheet of paper. This time, normal probability would allow you four correct guesses before any evidence of ESP can be claimed.

TUNING IN YOUR "MENTAL TELEVISION"— To update the experiments of author Upton Sinclair with his wife's "mental radio," you can have a friend co-operate in determining whether or not you can tune in your "mental television."

Without your knowledge of their subject matter, have a friend cut out a number of pictures from some magazines, probably half a dozen to start with. For best results these pictures should portray scenes of action and high emotional impact. A photograph of a burning building, an accident victim, and, lest we should be considered morbid, a happy child running in a meadow with a frisky puppy. Such photographs are readily obtainable among the news, features, and advertisements in any weekly newsmagazine.

While your friend acts as agent in one room, lie down on a couch or slouch in an easy chair in an attitude of complete relaxation. This experiment will take a good deal longer than the card-guessing tests, and both you and your agent should be prepared to exercise a considerable amount of patience.

No outside distractions should clutter up your concentration, and if you should decide to attempt this test on an evening when your friend has to catch a bus in an hour, you would be best advised to forget it for that night. Again, you, as the percipient, must not think! Conscious levels of your mind may feel obligated to exercise imagination in an earnest attempt to "guess" the subject matter of the photograph. You must learn to silence your sincere, but uninformed, levels of upper mind and allow your transcendent self to provide you with an accurate image of the photograph on which the agent is concentrating.

When you feel that a true picture has been formed in your mind, either jot down a description of the photograph or attempt your own sketch of the target material. Both the percipient and the agent must record the image at a previously agreed upon time of transmission.

This test may also be accomplished with free hand sketches, the agent originating the drawings and the percipient attempting to duplicate the sketch while in another room.

TESTING FOR EXTRA OCULAR VISION—Weekly newsmagazines will once again provide all the tools necessary for the testing of your EOV. Choose either covers or inside illustrations that have large areas of printed color, the brighter the better. Run your fingers over the spots of color and try to determine whether or not you can distinguish an individual "feeling" for each color. Next, attempt to distinguish the colors while blind-folded. You may be surprised to discover that one color may feel "sticky," another may feel "cool," and another may feel ridged or coarse. With practice, many people have become quite adept at "feeling" colors while blind-folded. Be certain that each color has been printed on the same texture of paper. Taking all samples from a single issue of a "slick" news weekly should provide maximum textural uniformity.

Parapsychologists have long observed the high inci-dence of ESP in children. Children have not yet acquired rigid patterns of thought and behavior and tend to ex-ercise rather than suppress their paranormal abilities.

In the Netherlands, Miss Nicky Louwrens, under the supervision of Dr. W. H. C. Tenhaeff, director of Utrecht's Parapsychology Institute, conducted a card guessing ex-periment with 1,188 Dutch children and their school-teachers. Her accumulated evidence seems to demon-strate what so many parents had already guessed thou-sands of generations ago: young children, especially those in the four-to-six age group, can do a remarkable job of reading grownups' minds. Average scores in card runs of twenty-five ran as high as fifteen hits, or 60% correct. Normal probability would allow only five hits per run, or 20% correct.

In 1937, Dr. Raleigh Drake of Wesleyan College in Macon, Georgia, investigated an eleven-year-old boy who was both mentally and physically retarded. When the boy's mother sat by his bedside and urged him to guess the cards that Dr. Drake held behind a screen in another room, the lad averaged 13.8 hits per run, then 21 hits per run, and finally attained a run with a perfect score of 25.

In 1936 two female researchers from Duke University conducted a test in a children's home and gave the children candy as incentive to co-operate in the experi-ment. Jokingly, one of the researchers announced that she would give a fifty-cent piece to any child who managed a perfect score. A girl named Lillian made 23. When the experimenters returned to the home, Lillian kept a promise that she had made and accomplished a perfect run of 25 hits.

You may find it interesting to test your child's ESP as well as your own. Zener cards, an ordinary pack of playing cards, or attractive pictures clipped from a magazine will all serve the purpose quite well. In the child's case, however, it would be best to have a duplicate set of the targets which you are using in the test. This is generally quite effective in working with the very young, because agent and percipient are each able to have a set of the cards in front of him. Also, I would recommend using only five cards instead of twenty-five. Here is a working procedure which you may follow, or, you may improvise one of your own.

Set your child at one end of the table with five cards face up before him, then, after erecting some sort of screen between you, seat yourself at the other end. Explain to the child that you want him to guess which card you are looking at whenever he hears you snap your fingers. Remember, the signal must not be a spoken one. Instruct him to look carefully at the cards before he tells you which one he thinks you are thinking about.

After you have snapped your fingers or given some other sort of unspoken sound signal, concentrate on one of the five cards placed face up in front of you. When the child tells you his guess, record whether or not it was a hit or a miss. Repeat the procedure five times for a complete run. As before, five hits are within normal probability. If your child should hit ten or more, control your excitement, but praise him and encourage him to try to do better on future "guessing games." Above all, do not tire him or bore him with the procedure.

These experiments may be attempted many times over —the more sessions, the better. Keep accurate records and average your scores together. Encourage friends with similar interests to engage in the experiments along with you. Compare your results. You may find that you possess your own private entryway into the world of ESP.